Crucial Questions
About
The Kingdom Of God

Crucial Questions About the Kingdom of God

The Sixth Annual Mid-Year Lectures of
Western Conservative Baptist Theological Seminary,
Portland, Oregon

by

GEORGE ELDON LADD

Professor of New Testament History and Biblical Theology
Fuller Theological Seminary

WM. B. EERDMANS PUBLISHING CO.

Grand Rapids   Michigan

Set up and printed, September, 1952

Fifth printing, February, 1968

ISBN 13: 978-0-8028-1571-2

To

MY MOTHER

Foreword

The Sixth Annual Mid-Year Lectures of Western Conservative Baptist Theological Seminary which are embodied in this book (together with some additional observations which the limited time for the lectures precluded) drew capacity attendances to the seminary chapel. Dr. Ladd's presence was much appreciated. His genial personality and fair presentation of controversial subjects lifted the meetings to a high level of Christian discussion. Some little time was spent after lecture hours with questioning students.

Some who read these pages will find questions rising in their minds. The subject considered has been divisive throughout the history of Biblical interpretation, and particularly during the current century. In these lectures Dr. Ladd constantly leads us to the Bible so that we might exercise the "more noble" Berean mind, "examining the scriptures daily whether these things were so." Though one's opinions differ the material here presented should be carefully evaluated.

Dr. Ladd, as a true evangelical believer in an inerrant Bible, has carefully weighed the relevant material on the subject in question. Though having a broader understanding of the kingdom than has been customary among most modern millennialists, the author strongly espouses the premillennial return of Christ.

One grand conviction basic to our faith and our Christian enterprise throbs through these pages. The teaching of the Scripture is, and the verdict of history will be — *Christus victor.*

Earl S. Kalland
Portland, Oregon

Preface

Both because of the frequency with which the idea of the Kingdom is referred to and elaborated upon by our Lord, and the vast literature which has proceeded from the discussion of the Kingdom of God in the church, especially in the nineteenth and twentieth centuries, every Christian and serious Bible student must acknowledge that here is a subject of major importance concerning which one should come to some definite conclusion. When a young man, I lived in an atmosphere (the very finest evangelical atmosphere in America, for which I shall be eternally grateful — I have often wondered what I would be doing today if I had been brought up, as millions are, in an environment of skepticism, in a home where the Scriptures were neither revered nor believed) in which I *thought* — and in this I may have been wrong — that one must not talk about any Kingdom of God as existing in our generation, for this was a theme that only liberals were preaching, and any statement pointing to the Kingdom must be placed at the end of this age. Let me repeat, I may have misinterpreted the things heard, but this was the feeling in my boyish heart. Since then I have learned to think differently, in fact, must even confess that I am compelled to disagree with many of my friends today who think that "the Kingdom" must not be mentioned except in relation to some distant event. I never heard anyone then discuss, for instance, the last verse of the Book of Acts, where we find Paul "preaching the kingdom of God and teaching the things concerning the Lord Jesus Christ." If Paul did not have the Gospel, and if he was not exclusively preaching the Gospel by the time he reached Rome for his first imprisonment, then I do not know when Paul ever had a Gospel. Furthermore, when our Lord said at the beginning of His ministry that unless a man was born again he could not enter the Kingdom of God, I believe He meant that everyone who is born again has entered the Kingdom of God, and that new birth brings him into that Kingdom. But there are other aspects of the Kingdom which many ignore. There is a Messianic Kingdom also to be set up on this earth. There will be a throne and a King upon it of the line of David, and there will also be a final consummation of this Kingdom. It is not my purpose in this preface to enter into these problems — and problems they are.

Multitudes of people in former generations, on the other hand, have been misled into believing that this gospel of the Kingdom can be interpreted exclusively in social and ethical terms, and many liberals have seized upon it and preached a message which utterly ignores the great central themes of the gospel of the Lord Jesus Christ. Such men as Albert Schweitzer have brought great confusion into the ranks of the church by their theories about Christ's teachings on the Kingdom. Almost all of the books now being written by recognized scholars in the English world relating to the problems of New Testament eschatology are written by men who have a liberal view of the Scriptures, who believe that our Lord was grossly mistaken in many of His statements, and who deny that there will be any ultimate earthly kingdom with Christ reigning here on earth. Even conservative scholars like Professor Berkhof of Calvin College, who fully embrace plenary inspiration, have misconstrued in part the New Testament doctrine of the Kingdom. I believe that Dr. Ladd's work is the first volume to appear in our country since the beginning of this century written by a thoroughly equipped scholar who knows the views of the principal New Testament scholars, who is well acquainted with the important literature in French, German, and English, and who at the same time is a thorough-going premillennialist, a believer in a Messianic Kingdom and in the millennium to come. For this reason, his book assumes major importance.

Inasmuch as this is the first book to be published by my friend and colleague, a word concerning the author is in order. George E. Ladd received his Bachelor of Theology degree from Gordon College of Theology and Missions, followed by a Bachelor of Divinity degree from Gordon Divinity School, Boston. After a year's study in classics in the Graduate School of Boston University, he began graduate work at Harvard University in the field of Biblical and Patristic Greek, including the history and literature of the intertestamental period, hellenistic backgrounds of the New Testament, and the history and criticism of the Greek Old and New Testaments. This was consummated in 1949 with a degree of Doctor of Philosophy in the Department of Classics at Harvard University. In addition, he engaged in special studies in the Episcopal Theological Seminary at Cambridge. Since 1950, Dr. Ladd has been Associate Professor of New Testament in the Fuller Theological Seminary, Pasadena. Through daily contact with him, and with the students of this seminary, I have come to know that he has a thorough mastery of the subjects which he teaches, that he has a deep passion and enthusiasm for these holy themes, and that his teaching is greatly appreciated by the student body.

In writing the preface to this book, I would like to make only one criticism. I think that Dr. Ladd, like many other writers on this subject, has not adequately pointed out the difference between the concept of the Kingdom of God in the New Testament and the Messianic Kingdom, the reign of Christ on this earth. They certainly are not synonymous terms. Dr. Ladd is contemplating a much larger work, covering the whole field of New Testament eschatology, and I am sure that in his subsequent volume this very important matter will be given more extensive consideration.

As an older man in this field of Biblical interpretation, especially in eschatology, with a great many friends in circles of extreme dispensationalism, whom I deeply love, may I ask for this young man a very careful hearing. His book is based upon thorough scholarship and unswerving loyalty to the Word of God. I think that it is time for all who believe the Holy Scriptures to be divinely inspired, who love the Lord's appearing, and who believe that only in His second advent is there any hope for this world, to approach these subjects without dogmatic pride, without a feeling that we ourselves have attained the last word, that there is nothing further to be said after we have expressed our convictions. If there is any body of people in this country prone to divide bitterly, it is the students of prophecy, who so quickly belabor others who do not agree with them in some points, as, for instance, the matter of whether the Church will go through the tribulation, the revival of the Roman Empire, the building of a millennial Temple in Jerusalem, the establishment of a Davidic throne on this earth, etc. But if there is one body of men who ought to be united in love for the Lord and His Word, it is this group.

I write this preface with pleasure. It is a joy to commend to all students of the inexhaustible, ever-fascinating and profoundly important area of Biblical predictive prophecy this carefully executed work of my beloved friend and colleague.

Wilbur M. Smith
Fuller Theological Seminary
Pasadena, California

Author's Foreword

The subject of the kingdom of God has presented a peculiar attraction to me for a number of years because of its prominent place in the teachings of our Lord and because of the great diversity of interpretation among equally devout students of the Word. Throughout college and seminary days, I adhered to the particular premillennial interpretation — usually called dispensationalism — which I had previously learned and attempted to find support for this position in the Scriptures and to familiarize myself with other important contemporary interpretations. While the current premillennial interpretation seemed more nearly to coincide with the New Testament teaching than any other, there remained a feeling of uncertainty as to the soundness of some of its positions. Accompanying this was a growing dissatisfaction with the quality of much of the literature which espoused this position. Most of the books I read seemed to assume the whole system rather than prove it. While many biblical passages were quoted, the exegetical problems involved appeared to me to be unsolved. The solution of these seemed to be essential to the consistency of the position.

In the course of graduate studies, I determined to go as deeply as possible into the backgrounds of biblical eschatology. In the past several years, I have made the kingdom of God, especially as it appears in the Gospels, the object of special study, intent on discovering an interpretation which would square with the apparently diverse New Testament data. This has led me to espouse positions which do not coincide with those with which many American Evangelicals are familiar and to differ with many students of the Word with whom I would prefer to agree. Nevertheless, I have tried to discover for myself what the New Testament in general and our Lord in particular teach about the kingdom of God, and without assuming any system at the outset, to make my way through the modern literature to whatever conclusions the biblical data might require. The measure of success which has been achieved in this quest will be for others to decide.

The invitation to lecture at the Western Conservative Baptist Theological Seminary provided the opportunity to reduce to writing some of my conclusions. These lectures deal only with a few of the basic questions and do not pretend to provide a systematic or a comprehensive exposition of the New Testament doctrine of the kingdom of God. I am fully aware that far more problems are left unanswered than are discussed, and many important passages of the New Testament remain untouched. The particular questions treated in the lectures were selected because of their relevance to the thinking of American Evangelicals. Within the necessary limitations, I have attempted to sketch against the background of these crucial questions some of the high-lights of the position to which the study of the Word of God has led me.

For the purposes of publication, each lecture has been divided into two chapters. With the exception of the last two chapters, the study is centered in our Lord's teachings, for the kingdom of God is one of the most central themes in his Evangel. It will appear to many to be a weakness that so little appeal is made to the Old Testament prophecies; but I am convinced that we must interpret the Old Testament by the New and not vice versa, and this procedure has been deliberately followed.

I wish to express my appreciation to Dr. Earl S. Kalland, President of Western Conservative Baptist Theological Seminary, and to the Faculty and student body for their kindly reception of the lectures. I am indebted to my colleagues, Dr. Wilbur M. Smith, Dr. Clarence S. Roddy, and Dr. Everett F. Harrison for reading the manuscript and offering many helpful suggestions.

George E. Ladd

Pasadena, California
March, 1952

Table of Contents

HAVE THE PROBLEMS ABOUT THE KINGDOM OF GOD BEEN SOLVED?

A Survey of the History of Interpretation

Outline

THE ANCIENT AND MEDIEVAL PERIOD
The eschatological interpretation
The non-eschatological interpretation

THE MODERN PERIOD
Non-eschatological interpretations
The eschatological interpretation of Consistent Eschatology
Non-eschatological interpretations since Schweitzer
Realized eschatology
The search for a synthesis

CHAPTER I

Have the Problems About the Kingdom
of God Been Solved?

THE STUDY of the kingdom of God in the New Testament has evoked many difficult questions. Is the kingdom present or future? Is it a spiritual, inner reality, or is it a kingdom to be manifested apocalyptically? Is it the present reign of God in the hearts of men, or is it a future reign of Christ on earth? Can it be both? If the kingdom is future, in what sense can it be a present spiritual reality? What is the relationship of the kingdom of God in the Gospels to the Old Testament kingdom prophecies? Why does Matthew speak about the kingdom of God and the kingdom of heaven?

Questions like these, apparently quite simple, have challenged students of biblical theology with their difficulty. They are still live issues in contemporary biblical study and even today receive very diverse answers from different schools of thought.

The study of any field of biblical theology must ever relate itself to the history of interpretation. Unless a man can evaluate and criticize his own position in the light of the history of Christian thought, he is unlikely to achieve a sound balance in the maintenance of his position. This is particularly true of eschatology and the kingdom of God. It is easy to accept an inherited position uncritically and to espouse it dogmatically; but scholarship, even though it may achieve theological positions which are maintained dogmatically, must continually purify itself by the criticisms of others and criticize itself in the light of all the findings of theological studies.

As we approach the question of the meaning of the kingdom of God, it is necessary to orientate our study to the history of the doctrine that we may understand the background for the various contemporary interpretations and may thereby evaluate more accurately the soundness of our own conclusions. While it is true that "the history of the attempt to answer this question is the history of Christian thought from the very beginning of time to the present day,"[1] we may nevertheless sketch in brief outline the interpretations of the kingdom in Christian theology which have exercised the greatest influence. Such a sketch will reveal that the problems have not reached final solution and that the kingdom of God in the New Testament deserves fresh study.

THE ANCIENT AND MEDIEVAL PERIOD

The eschatological interpretation

In the early church two interpretations of the kingdom are to be found: an eschatological interpretation and a non-eschatological interpretation. During the first two centuries the kingdom of God in the Church Fathers was exclusively eschatological. A typical passage is found in the *Didache*: "Remember, Lord, thy Church, to . . . gather it together in its holiness from the four winds to thy kingdom which thou hast prepared for it."[2] The church is the present visible people of God on earth, but the kingdom is the future realm of blessedness to be experienced after the return of Christ to the earth.

Sometimes this eschatological kingdom is more specifically defined. In several of the early Fathers the kingdom involved

---

1. F. C. Burkitt, *The Interpreter*, VII (1910-11), pp. 145-6.
2. *The Didache* X, 5. Tr. by K. Lake, *The Apostolic Fathers* (*The Loeb Classical Library*) London: Heinemann, 1930, I, p. 325.

an earthly millennial reign of Christ. This is clearly stated by such writers as Barnabas (XV), Papias (in Irenaeus *Adv. Haer.*, V, 33), Justin Martyr (*Dial.* LXXX), Irenaeus (*Adv. Haer.* V, 33-35) and Tertullian (*De res. carn.* XXV, *Adv. Marcion*, III, 25)[3]. Other early Fathers do not make it clear whether they believed in a future temporal earthly kingdom or not. However, a survey of the literature leads to the following conclusions. The understanding of the kingdom is exclusively eschatological; and with one exception there is no Church Father before Origen who opposed the millenarian interpretation, and there is no one before Augustine whose extant writings offer a different interpretation of Revelation 20 than that of a future earthly kingdom consonant with the natural interpretation of the language.[4]

The non-eschatological interpretation

The non-eschatological interpretation of the kingdom arose with Origen and Augustine. Origen is famous for his allegorical method of interpreting the Bible. To him Scripture was to be understood in a three-fold way: the somatic, or the natural, literal; the psychic, or moral, which had to do with the directions for human conduct; and the pneumatic, or the spiritual, which had to do with the deeper truths of the spiritual world. In the application of the spiritual method

---

3. Cf. A. Harnack, "Millennium," *Encyclopaedia Britannica*, 9th ed.; XVI, pp. 328-9; D. H. Kromminga, *The Millennium in the Church* (Grand Rapids: Eerdmans, 1945) pp. 29-64; Lèon Gry, *Le millénairisme dans ses origines et son développement* (Paris: Picard, 1904). Kromminga attempts to prove that Barnabas did not anticipate an earthly millennium, but to the present writer he has not succeeded. It is worth noting that Berkhof includes Barnabas as a supporter of a millennium (*The Kingdom of God*, Grand Rapids: Eerdmans, 1951, p. 21).

4. Aside from a small sect known as the Alogi, (cf. Th. Zahn, "Alogi," *The New Schaff-Herzog Encyclopedia*, I, p. 135) the one known exception is Caius, a Roman ecclesiastic of about 200 A. D. who reacted strongly against the eschatological excesses of the Montanists. In his anti-Montanist polemic, he attributed the source of Chiliasm to the heretic Cerinthus (Eusebius, *H. E.*, III, xxviii, 2) rather than to the Scriptures. Cf. below, pp. 154 ff., for a further discussion of the eschatology of the early church.

of interpretation Origen employed allegorism, refusing to admit in many portions of Scripture any natural or literal significance.   By this free method of exegesis he eliminated the future realistic eschatological kingdom, labeling such an interpretation as "Jewish."[5]

Another type of interpretation was introduced by Augustine. This great theologian at first espoused the natural interpretation of Revelation 20 concerning the kingdom of God as a future literal reign of Christ with his saints on earth.[6] However, Augustine reacted against the gross sensual interpretation of contemporary chiliasts, and in the course of working out his concept of the City of God, he came to identify the church and the kingdom of God and to explain the millennium in Revelation 20 as representing Christian experience when Christ raises the believing soul from a state of spiritual death to share his spiritual life and so to reign with him.[7]

While it is possible that others before him may have held this view, Augustine was the first who ventured to teach that the Catholic Church was the kingdom of Christ and the City of God, and that the millennial kingdom had begun with the first appearing of Christ and therefore was to have no future fulfillment.

While it is debatable whether Augustine identified the kingdom of God with the true church, i.e., with the body of genuine believers in Christ, or with the visible ecclesiastical hierarchy of the Roman Church,[8] it is quite clear that medieval thought understood the kingdom in terms of the visible, ecclesiastical system.   Augustine's doctrine of the City of God banished the millennial interpretation of the kingdom from the realm of dogmatic Catholic theology.

----

5. *De Principiis* II, xi, 2-3.
6. Cf. *Sermones* 259, 2 in Migne, *Patrologia Latina*, XXXVIII, p. 1197.
7. *City of God* XX, 6-10, especially 9.
8. Cf. Chapter V in Archibald Robertson, *Regnum Dei* (New York: Macmillan, 1901).

The Reformers did not depart drastically from the Augustinian concept of the kingdom. While they did not articulate a clear-cut doctrine, "they agreed in identifying it with the invisible Church, the community of the elect, or of the saints of God."[9] The kingdom was to them the reign of God in the hearts of the redeemed and was therefore essentially a religious concept and primarily a present reality.

THE MODERN PERIOD

Non-eschatological interpretations

As we come to modern times we may again divide the interpretation of the kingdom of God into eschatological and non-eschatological views. The most influential non-eschatological interpretation stems from the theological views of Albert Ritschl (1822-1889). In his theology, the kingdom of God is one of the most central doctrines, and sometimes it seems to be the dominating idea.[10]

However, the kingdom is not an eschatological concept nor is it the church, whether defined as the ecclesiastical system or the body of true believers. The kingdom is "the organization of humanity through action inspired by love,"[11] "the moral unification of the human race, through action prompted by universal love to our neighbour,"[12] "the association of men for reciprocal and common action from the motive of love."[13] This conception of the kingdom can hardly be equated with the New Testament teaching. It ignores the uniform biblical emphasis that the kingdom is utterly supernatural, the activity of God (Mark 4:26-29) and not the product of human interaction. It changes the center of emphasis from that of a religious focus, viz., the reign of God, to an ethical principle,

9. L. Berkhof, *op. cit.*, p. 24 and references cited there.
10. Cf. L. Berkhof, *op. cit.*, p. 31.
11. Albrecht Ritschl, *The Christian Doctrine of Justification and Reconciliation* (E.T., New York: Scribner's, 1900) p. 12.
12. *Ibid.*, p. 280.
13. *Ibid.*, p. 290.

the motivation of love. It neglects the inescapable eschatological aspect of the kingdom in the New Testament (Matt. 13:39-43).

Nevertheless, Ritschl served to call attention anew to the theological significance of the kingdom of God and to stimulate study of the concept. He made it a principle at work in the world of men within the scene of human history. This was a new departure from former views, and it provided the background for the social conception of the kingdom which was so very prominent a few decades ago and which is still greatly influential.[14] This Ritschlian interpretation of Christianity as a spiritual religion with ethical ends which were to be attained gradually by a united community was well adapted to the evolutionary optimism which characterized the last of the nineteenth century.[15] Contemporary church programs which emphasize the goal of "building the kingdom of God" manifest the persisting influence of this interpretation of the kingdom as a social ideal. For our present purpose it will be unnecessary to deal further with this view for it departs so completely from the New Testament teaching about the kingdom that few New Testament scholars today would espouse it as representing the New Testament idea.

Ritschl's view of a non-eschatological kingdom of God exercised a far-reaching influence in the last half of the nineteenth century and may be traced in the thinking of New Testament scholars who have interpreted the kingdom of God primarily as a present spiritual reality. Harnack's popular lectures delivered in 1899-1900 provide a classic illustration.[16] He viewed the kingdom as the rule of the holy God in the

---

14. Cf. the excellent analysis and critical evaluation of this social concept of the kingdom in Berkhof, *op. cit.*, chapters VI to VIII.

15. C. C. McCown, *The Search for the Real Jesus* (New York: Scribner's, 1940), p. 226.

16. *What is Christianity?* (New York: Putnam's, 1901. E. T. of *Das Wesen Christentums*, Leipzig: Hinrich, 1900).

hearts of individuals, the power that works inwardly. "The kingdom of God comes by coming to the individual, by entering into his soul and laying hold of it" (p. 60). The eschatological, apocalyptic language in the Gospels is the "husk" which contains the kernel of spiritual truth. The husk must be cast aside but the kernel retained. The kingdom is entirely a matter of God and the soul. This teaching about the kingdom dominated Jesus' message. "Everything else that he proclaimed can be brought into connection with this" (p. 68).

The influence of Ritschl's view may be seen in scholars more conservative than Harnack. A. B. Bruce[17] interpreted the kingdom as the "highest good of life" in which the Fatherliness of God for men and the sonship of man for God is realized in a spiritual universal kingdom; and this ideal was to be realized in the new people of God as the kingdom is assigned to a positive locality, the church (pp. 60-62, 265). Bruce practically eliminates any realistic eschatology, interpreting apocalyptic traits as symbols and figures of spiritual truths. His concept has essentially much in common with Ritschl's when he says, "All who live in the spirit of love the Son of Man recognizes as Christians unawares, and therefore as heirs of the kingdom" (p. 318).

One of the most vigorous opponents of the Ritschlian theology and its subjectivism was James Orr, staunch contender for the evangelical faith. Yet in his interpretation of the kingdom of God, he embodied elements which are strikingly similar to Ritschl's view. Orr restored the religious center of the kingdom, which Ritschl missed, by making it the reign of God; and his understanding of how God exercises his reign in the hearts of men would be vastly different from Harnack's. Nevertheless he sees the kingdom as a new

---

17. *The Kingdom of God; or, Christ's Teaching According to the Synoptical Gospels* (Edinburgh: T. and T. Clark, 1890).

principle, the rule of God in human hearts, established in human society by Christ and designed to transform it in all its relations.[18] The new principle of God's reign works from within outwards for the renewal and transformation of every department of our earthly existence such as marriage, the family, the state, social life, etc.[19] From the gospel of the kingdom has gone forth a regenerating center into art, culture, philosophy, politics, commerce, education, science, literature, economics and social reform, and when all of these areas of life have been brought under the control of God's will, his kingdom will have come. Orr, like Bruce, views the eschatological element in the Gospels as symbolic of spiritual realities. The Parousia is a series of crises in human history by which God's kingdom is promoted,[20] and thus the kingdom slowly develops, both by gradual development and sharp crises.[21]

------

18. James Orr, "The Kingdom of God" *Hastings Dictionary of the Bible*, II, pp. 844-856; "The Idea of the Kingdom of God," *The Christian View of God and the World* (New York: Scribner's, 1897), pp. 349-361; cf. also *The Ritschlian Theology and the Evangelical Faith* (London: Hodder and Stoughton, 1898), *passim*.

19. *H. D. B.*, II, p. 852.

20. *Ibid.*, p. 854. Orr does not mean to deny the personal second, coming of Christ. Cf. *Sidelights on Christian Doctrine* (London: Marshall Bros., 1909), pp. 105ff.

21. Cf. for a similar view V. H. Stanton, "The Teaching of Jesus concerning the Kingdom of God" in *The Jewish and the Christian Messiah* (Edinburgh: T. and T. Clark, 1886), pp. 203-225; and James S. Candlish *The Kingdom of God Biblically and Historically Considered* (Edinburgh: T. and T. Clark, 1884). To Candlish the kingdom is "the gathering together of men, under God's eternal law of righteous love, by the vital power of his redeeming love in Jesus Christ, brought to bear upon them through the Holy Spirit" (p. 197). Candlish holds that the Parousia of Christ for judgment will occur at the end of the development of the messianic kingdom, instead of at the beginning, as the Old Testament prophets seemed to indicate (p. 167).

The far-reaching extent of Ritschl's influence may be seen in that his distinction between the kingdom and the church — the moral and the religious aspects of the same community of men — was adopted by Candlish, (*op. cit.*, pp. 205, 404) and Professor Oswald T. Allis (*Prophecy and the Church*, Philadelphia: The Presbyterian and Reformed Pub. Co., 1945, pp. 83-4).

The eschatological interpretation of Consistent Eschatology

A turning point in the study of the kingdom of God came with Johannes Weiss[22] and Albert Schweitzer.[23] These two scholars espoused a new type of interpretation of the kingdom which has come to be known as "consistent eschatology." According to this view, the kingdom in the teaching of Jesus was altogether eschatological. To interpret it as a present spiritual reality in any sense is to import an element which was not in Jesus' mind. His message was consistent and thorough-going eschatology. The kingdom was entirely a future apocalyptic reality which would come by a miraculous intrusion of God to terminate human history and inaugurate the kingdom. By various exegetical devices, Weiss discounts the natural meaning of sayings of Jesus which seem to represent the kingdom as already present.

As important as this purely eschatological interpretation *per se* is the correlative view propounded by Weiss and Schweitzer that Jesus expected this apocalyptic kingdom to come *in his own lifetime*. The end was at hand; the coming of the kingdom was near; it was about to come and interrupt the normal course of human existence; the Messianic Age was immediately to dawn. Therefore, men must be possessed by one concern and one only: to prepare for the end. This expectation of an imminent end of the world determined the character of Jesus' ethical teaching. He did not give his disciples a body of ethical instruction designed to be normative for human conduct in the ordinary course of experience. On the contrary, because the time was so short and ordinary human experience was so soon to be terminated, a special

---

22. *Die Predigt Jesu vom Reiche Gottes* (Göttingen: Vandenhoeck und Ruprecht, 1892; zweite Auflage, 1900).

23. *The Mystery of the Kingdom of God* (London: Black, 1925. E. T. of second part of *Das Abendmahl*, Tübingen: Mohr, 1901); and *Von Reimarus zu Wrede* (Tübingen: Mohr, 1906); E. T. *The Quest of the Historical Jesus* (London: Black, 1945; first printed in 1910). See especially the last book, pp. 349-395.

ethic was demanded. The ordinary pursuits of life and the commonly accepted standards were inadequate. Nothing mattered except preparedness for the impending end. This ethic has been called an "interim ethic," i.e., a temporary expedient designed to be used only for the brief interim before the world should end.

It is obvious that if Jesus had such an expectation, he was mistaken. The world did not come to an end. The kingdom did not come. The one to whom the Christian church looks as the source of its life, faith, and inspiration, was in fact a deluded fanatic, a man who died because his faith was set upon wild apocalyptic dreams.

This consistent or thorough-going eschatology is one of the most influential interpretations in modern times in liberal New Testament studies. It is obvious that such a view is devastating to the traditional Christology and to any high view of the inspiration of the Scriptures. The quest for the "historical" Jesus is for Schweitzer a quest for one who shared the apocalyptic views of his contemporaries, and who historically was a human figure and nothing more. Nevertheless, many scholars have accepted this consistent eschatology and have attempted to work out its implications in the whole realm of the life and teachings of Jesus,[24] while others have written commentaries which are greatly indebted to this point of view.[25]

Several monographs defending this position are particularly important. E. F. Scott was one of the first to undertake a

24. Cf. F. C. Burkitt, *Jesus Christ-An Historical Outline* (London: Blackie, 1932) : J. Warschauer, *The Historical Life of Christ* (New York: Macmillan, 1926) ; Charles Guignebert, *Jesus* (New York: Knopf, 1935), especially pp. 325-352; B. S. Easton, *Christ in the Gospels* (New York: Scribner's, 1930), pp. 154-164.

25. Cf. A. H. McNeile, *The Gospel According to St. Matthew* (London: Macmillan, 1915); W. C. Allen, *A Critical and Exegetical Commentary on the Gospel According to St. Matthew* (New York: Scribner's, 1913).

comprehensive exposition of the kingdom of God in the New Testament along these lines. In his book *The Kingdom and the Messiah*,[26] he was so convinced of the correctness of Weiss' and Schweitzer's position that he could say, "Criticism is gradually settling toward the conviction that the apocalyptic element is not merely accidental to our Lord's teaching, but is all-pervading and determinative."[27] Scott attempted to maintain the permanent validity of the Christian Gospel while following the admittedly one-sided emphasis of consistent eschatology. His book is one of the most lucid and stimulating presentations of this point of view to be found.

This same position is argued in exegetical detail in a more recent book by Wm. Michaelis entitled *The Baptist, Jesus, and the Early Church. The Message of the Kingdom of God Before and After Pentecost.*[28] Michaelis begins with the passages in the Gospels which describe the kingdom in eschatological terms and, taking this emphasis as the necessary point of departure, interprets other "neutral" passages in such a way that they do not contradict the eschatological aspect, but even support it.[29] Michaelis insists that those who find any present kingdom in Jesus' teachings do so because they read it into various passages in the Gospels. With Jesus the kingdom possessed only an *endzeitlichen* character.[30] Michaelis

26. Edinburgh: T. and T. Clark, 1911.

27. *Op. cit.*, p. v. In a later work, *The Kingdom of God in the New Testament* (New York: Macmillan, 1931), Scott radically modified his earlier position by recognizing that the kingdom in Jesus' teaching was not only future and apocalyptic but was also a present reality. He makes no reference, however, to his earlier position.

It should be noted that in his earlier book, Scott did not follow consistent eschatology in its interpretation of Jesus' ethics as only "interim." Jesus' ethic was an ideal ethic, even though set in an apocalyptic framework.

28. *Täufer, Jesus, Urgemeinde. Die Predigt vom Reiche Gottes vor und nach Pfingsten* (Gütersloh: Bertelsman, 1928).

29. *Ibid.*, p. 64.

30. *Ibid.*, p. 82.

feels that the resurrection and pentecostal experiences of the early church modified the eschatological unity of Jesus' message about the kingdom. These experiences have necessitated a reinterpretation of the kingdom, and it is now to be understood as a present reality as well as a future expectation.

Martin Werner has taken consistent eschatology as a point of departure for an interpretation of the history of dogma. He affirms that Jesus taught only a future, apocalyptic, imminent kingdom,[31] and that the early history of dogma is to be found in the reaction of the early Christian church to the delay of the expected imminent Parousia of Christ and the coming of the kingdom.

Non-eschatological interpretations since Schweitzer

Not all critics have accepted the validity of the position of consistent eschatology, and various techniques have been employed to minimize the importance of the eschatological element or to set it aside altogether. Some scholars, like von Dobschütz,[32] admitted the presence of eschatology in the teachings of Jesus but insisted that it is not the essential element in the Gospel and therefore might be ignored; the non-eschatological element is the essential factor in Jesus' message.

Lewis Muirhead,[33] following Erich Haupt,[34] recognized that Jesus believed in a futuristic aspect of the kingdom; but they insist that the apocalyptic elements are pictures from which realities cannot be deduced. The future aspect of the kingdom did not dominate Jesus' thought, for the kingdom is already

31. *Die Entstehung des christlichen Dogmas* (Bern and Leipzig: Haupt, 1941), pp. 36-74.
32. *The Eschatology of the Gospels* (London: Hodder and Stoughton, 1910).
33. *The Eschatology of Jesus, or The Kingdom Come and Coming* (New York: Armstrong, 1904).
34. *Die eschatologischen Aussagen Jesu in den synoptischen Evangelien* (Berlin: Reuther and Reichard, 1895).

present in the inner experience of faith and the eschatology must be interpreted in keeping with this essential truth.[35]

Another way of eliminating the apocalyptic element is to delete it by critical excision. Wellhausen, famed for his Old Testament criticism, attributed the eschatological element in the Gospels to the primitive church rather than to Jesus. Jesus' teaching was non-eschatological, but when the early church came to believe he was the Messiah, it put the eschatological teachings which we find in our gospel records into his mouth.[36] Similarly H. B. Sharman[37] in a detailed critical study of the gospel records concludes that Jesus' message affirmed the kingdom of God to be present in his own ministry as God's mind was expressed through him and a new influence mediated through his personality upon others. Jesus forecast the destruction of Jerusalem and the wide-spread growth of the kingdom which had come in his ministry, and he sought to warn his disciples against messianic claimants who would arise at the time of war. The disciples neglected his warnings, and thus the genuine sayings of Jesus about the present kingdom suffered modifications and additions of an eschatological sort which must be sifted out as unauthentic. The kingdom in Jesus is purely a present spiritual reality; the eschatological elements in our Gospels are due to his disciples, not to Jesus.

---

35. A more recent presentation of a similar view is to be found in E. J. Goodspeed's *A Life of Jesus* (New York: Harper, 1950). According to Dr. Goodspeed, Jesus came to establish the reign of God on earth, in the hearts of men. The kingdom was not to be postponed to a future day, but was to be personally realized as men accepted the wealth of God's great love, and so began to live as individuals under the sway of the kingdom of God (p. 84). Apocalyptic was "his bold, imaginative way of asserting the certain triumph of the kingdom of God he was establishing . . ." (p. 127). Apocalyptic language is to be recognized as an Oriental mode of speech and is not to be taken literally (pp. 188-9).

36. *Einleitung in die drei ersten Evangelien* (Zweite Aufl.; Berlin: Reimer, 1911), pp. 79-104.

37. *The Teaching of Jesus About the Future* (Chicago: University Press, 1909), pp. 301-327. Cf. also *Son of Man and Kingdom of God* (New York: Harper, 1943).

Historical criticism is employed by F. C. Grant to set aside the eschatological element of the kingdom.[38] Grant feels that Jesus stands in the prophetic rather than the apocalyptic tradition in his conception of the kingdom; his concept was centered in his conception of God as Father. His message was essentially one of social redemption in which the divine sovereignty would be perfectly realized here on earth. He expected to see the reign of God established in Palestine (and everywhere on earth) in his own lifetime (p. 16). The social gospel is the original gospel of Jesus. The early Christians transformed his concept in an eschatological apocalyptic direction. This apocalyptic element cannot be attributed to Jesus, for any human being who would identify himself with the Son of Man coming from heaven in glory to establish an apocalyptic kingdom "could suggest little else than an unsound mind — certainly not the supreme and unquestioned sanity of the Man of Galilee" (p. 63). The early Christians interpreted Jesus in the light of Jewish apocalyptic symbols. Jesus was "certainly no mad fanatic, no deluded pretender to a celestial and really mythical title, no claimant to a throne which did not exist, no prophet of a coming judgment to be carried out by a heavenly figure seated on the clouds with whom he identified himself — which judgment never took place, never could take place" (pp. 67-8).

Realized eschatology

An entirely different type of eschatology but one which equally sets aside the apocalyptic element is found in "realized eschatology." C. H. Dodd, with whom the position has come to be identified, in his book, *The Parables of the Kingdom,*[39] takes as his point of departure the parables and sayings of Jesus which he interprets as teaching that the kingdom of God *had come.* The kingdom of God "is proclaimed as a present fact,

---

38. *The Gospel of the Kingdom* (New York: Macmillan, 1940).
39. *London*: Nisbet, 1935.

which men must recognize, whether by their actions they accept or reject it" (p. 44). The kingdom, according to Dodd, is present in this sense: "The *eschaton* has moved from the future to the present, from the sphere of expectation into that of realized experience" (p. 50). In this interpretation Jesus' view of the kingdom was not future at all but is to be understood as the entrance of the Absolute, the "wholly other," into the world of time and space (p. 107). The kingdom of God means that the Absolute has entered the sphere of history, the Eternal has come into time. "The predictions of Jesus have no long historical perspective. They seem to be concerned with the immediate developments of the crisis which was already in being when He spoke, and which he interpreted as the coming of the Kingdom of God" (pp. 108-9). They are "eschatological" in the sense that they deal with supra-sensible, supra-historical realities. The apocalyptic element is really to be taken symbolically (p. 105); but the early church interpreted it literally. Thus there arose the belief in two events, one past in Jesus' life, death and resurrection, and one future: his coming in the clouds; whereas Jesus referred actually to only a single event (p. 101).[40]

The search for a synthesis

A number of recent studies of the kingdom of God have sought for some clue by which the kingdom in Jesus' teachings could be understood in an eschatological, futuristic sense,

40. A similar view will be found in R. Bultmann, *Jesus and the Word* (New York: Scribner's, 1934. E. T. of *Jesus*, Berlin: Deutsche Bibliothek, 1926), where Jesus' teaching about the kingdom is innocent of the whole content of apocalyptic and dramatic eschatology, but consists of the transcendent event which brings man face to face with God and demands decision (pp. 39-41). The last hour is the "Now" in which a decision is demanded for God and against the world (p. 131).

The influence of realized eschatology may be seen in such books as A. M. Hunter, *The Work and Words of Jesus* (London: Student Christian Movement Press, 1950), pp. 68-79; William Manson, *Jesus the Messiah* (Philadelphia: Westminster Press, 1946), pp. 205-210; R. V. G. Tasker, *The Nature and Purpose of the Gospels* (London: Student Christian Movement Press, 1944), chapter VI.

and at the same time full force given to the gospel sayings in which the kingdom is a present reality.

G. Gloege in his book *The Kingdom of God and the Church in the New Testament*[41] takes as his point of departure modern philological study of *basileia*. From these data he insists that *basileia* always bears the abstract meaning "reign," and is never concretized into "realm" or "people." The kingdom of God is God's kingly activity for man's redemption. The kingdom is future and eschatological, but it is also present because the future reign is manifested in the present age, and because the reign of God is manifested in the mighty works of Jesus. The kingdom is not the church, for the kingdom is the rule of God while the church is a society of men. Yet the kingdom calls a society into being; God's rule envisages a community of the ruled, and creates it.

A similar solution is suggested by H. D. Wendland in *The Eschatology of the Kingdom of God according to Jesus.*[42] Wendland finds the solution in Jesus' thought about God and in his mission. The kingdom, God's rule, has both a futuristic (*Endzeitlichkeit*) and a transcendent quality (*Uberzeitlichkeit*). There is an inner polarity between the eschatology and transcendence of the kingdom which gives reality to the present sense of the kingdom. The transcendent kingdom has broken into the present world order demanding decision of men, but it will not be inherited until after the final judgment when this age is displaced by the age to come. The transcendent kingdom was present in Jesus, who was the Messiah; but his messianic work will not be complete until the future kingdom comes. Jesus was both the present and the future

---

41. *Das Reich Gottes und Kirche im Neuen Testament* (Gütersloh: Bertelsmann, 1929).

42. *Die Eschatologie des Reiches Gottes bei Jesus* (Gütersloh: Bertelsmann, 1931).

Messiah, and in him and his messianic activity, the kingdom was both present and future.

An interpretation which contains similar elements is to be found in Rudolf Otto's influential book on the kingdom of God.[43] Here the kingdom in Jesus' teachings is viewed always as a future eschatological kingdom which will follow the messianic woes and the final judgment. Yet the kingdom of God came to man in the person and mission of Jesus because an eschatological drama had taken place in heaven in which God had achieved a victory over Satan. Otto finds this by interpreting such passages as Matthew 12:25-29, Luke 10:18; 11:21, and Revelation 12:7 in the light of Iranian mythology. Since God has hurled Satan down from heaven, the kingdom of God has dawned, and the proof of it is the exorcism of demons. However, Jesus does not bring the kingdom, rather the kingdom brings Jesus with it. His person and work are part of the redemptive event which comes to men because Satan has been overthrown in heaven. Jesus knew himself to be the organ of the present coming of this eschatological order which was breaking into the world for salvation.[44]

There are several other outstanding recent studies on Jesus' eschatology and the kingdom of God which recognize the kingdom as both present and future. W. G. Kümmel has written a valuable study entitled *Promise and Fulfillment*[45] in which he represents Jesus as having expected that the kingdom in an eschatological form would come within a generation, but that Jesus also saw the kingdom as a reality already

---

43. *The Kingdom of God and The Son of Man* (Grand Rapids. Zondervan, 1938. E. T. of *Reich Gottes und Menschensohn,* München: Beck, 1934).

44. Dodd claims Otto's support for his "realized eschatology" (*The Parables of the Kingdom,* p. 49). However, Otto recognizes continually the realistic eschatology of the kingdom, while Dodd's view of the kingdom as completely realized empties it of any futuristic reality.

45. *Verheissung und Erfüllung. Untersuchungen zur eschatologischen Verkündigung Jesu* (Basel: H. Majer, 1945). Cf. also *Die Eschatologie der Evangelien* (Leipzig: Hinrichs, 1936).

present in his own person. Jesus expected that he would be
the judge in the future glorious kingdom; but since he was
already among men, their reaction to him, the earthly Jesus,
would be the basis for their judgment by the eschatological
Jesus of the future. The kingdom was thus already at work
in his person, activity and preaching. Therefore acceptance
of Jesus meant in effect acceptance of the future kingdom. In
Jesus the kingdom had begun, and in him it would be consummated (pp. 94-5).

C. J. Cadoux,[46] while admitting the presence of realistic
eschatology in Jesus' teaching, follows essentially the older
interpretation. He understands the kingdom in Jesus' teaching as the reign of God, but also as a society of human
beings, a growing society. The kingdom is on earth and will
grow as the number of its members increases. The essence
of the kingdom is a filial relation to God: the kingdom exists
wherever and whenever man submits in filial relation to God.
Jesus was the obedient son *par excellence;* therefore he
embodies the kingdom in his own person. Cadoux admits that
Jesus also looked forward to a cataclysmic coming of the
kingdom in the future when it would reach the triumphant
completion of its process of growth (p. 133). Jesus thought
he would depart to Paradise after his death, and shortly after
the destruction of Jerusalem which he anticipated, he would
return to earth in glory in the consummated kingdom. Cadoux
faces frankly the various efforts to equate these eschatological
expectations with the modern mind and concludes that one is
forced to affirm simply that Jesus was wrong in his eschatological expectations (pp. 338-347). However, the loss of
eschatology, in Cadoux's judgment, would not impair the
essence of Jesus' message of the kingdom. Furthermore,
Jesus' error was only in the *form* he expected his triumph to

---

46. *The Historic Mission of Jesus. A Constructive Re-examination of the
Eschatological Teaching in the Synoptic Gospels* (New York: Harper, n.d.)

take; it does not affect the triumph as such which is seen in the rise of the church.[47]

It is evident from this survey of recent studies on the kingdom of God by critical scholars that no single interpretation has established itself so firmly as to command universal recognition. Great advances have been made since the time of Ritschl, but the study of the kingdom of God continues to challenge the best thought in liberal circles.

---

47. Cf. for similar conclusions in other recent treatments which recognize both the present and the future elements in the kingdom *A. N. Wilder, Eschatology and Ethics in the Teaching of Jesus* (Revised edition; New York: Harper, 1950), pp. 50-52; Oscar Cullmann, *Christ and Time* (Philadelphia: The Westminster Press, 1950. E. T. of *Christus und die Zeit,* Zürich: Evangelischer Verlag, 1946), pp. 81-93; Jean Héring, *Le Royaume de Dieu et sa venu* (Paris: Felix Alcan, 1937), chapter III.

CHAPTER TWO

CONSERVATIVE INTERPRETATIONS OF THE KINGDOM OF GOD

Outline

CHAPTER II

Conservative Interpretations of the Kingdom of God

THE interpretation of the kingdom of God in modern times as it was traced in the first chapter dealt largely with the liberal wing of biblical studies. Until the rise of modern liberal criticism, scholars had looked upon the Bible as the inspired Word of God, Christ as the Son of God incarnate for man's redemption, and the teachings of Christ and of the Bible, therefore, as normative for theological thought as well as religious experience. However, in the last hundred years or more there has arisen a strong reaction to the traditional concept of Christian theology, and rationalistic and naturalistic philosophies rather than the Christian world-view found in the Scriptures have provided the intellectual framework within which much biblical scholarship has been carried forward. The Bible has come to be studied merely as an ancient historical and religious record rather than as the inspired Word of God. The tacit assumption, if not always the explicit affirmation of such scholarship, is that Jesus is to be studied as a human being possessing all of the limitations which are common to man. Indeed, Albert Schweitzer asserts that his consistent eschatology arises from the "thoroughgoing application of Jewish eschatology to the interpretation of the teaching and work of Jesus";[1] i.e., from the assumption that Jesus

---

1. *Paul and His Interpreters* (E. T., London: Black, 1912), p. ix.

historically was nothing more than a first century Jew who shared in full the apocalyptic views of his contemporaries.[2]

Many scholars who have been known as conservatives have been greatly influenced by the modern "critical" study of Jesus and his eschatology, and have gone along with the whole trend of critical liberal scholarship. Those who have felt obliged to accept the conclusion that Jesus was deluded by a false hope of the imminent end of the world, or who have felt it necessary to employ the techniques of literary or historical criticism to set aside the apocalyptic element have thereby abandoned a conservative attitude toward the Scriptures. Unfortunately, students who have retained a conservative view have often gone to the other extreme of ignoring altogether the problems raised by "critical" scholarship.[3]   There has not appeared

---

2. An excellent analysis of the history of this modern study of Jesus will be found in C. C. McCown, *The Search for the Real Jesus* (New York: Scribner's, 1940). McCown shows clearly how the successive philosophical movements from the rationalism of Strauss to the assumptions of the modern scientific method have molded the search for the "real," i. e., for the human Jesus.

3. It is unfortunate that the very word "critical" has come to be identified with only one branch of biblical and theological studies: the liberal and rationalistic wing. This use of the word is so fixed in our thinking that Webster's dictionary defines biblical criticism as follows: "Designating, or pertaining to, that school of Bible students who treat the received text with greater freedom than the Traditionalists do, discussing its sources and history and departing in many places from the traditional conclusion." This is the common but nevertheless inaccurate limitation of the term. In fact, again to quote the dictionary, criticism properly speaking is "the scientfic investigation of the origin, text, composition, character, history, etc., of literary documents, especially the Bible." The present writer would deny that scientific study of the Scriptures necessarily leads to the usually accepted "critical" positions. It is more accurate to speak of "liberal" criticism and "conservative" criticism, indicating by the two terms the philosophical assumptions which underly the study of the Scriptures. No man is free from philosophical presuppositions. One man may derive his assumptions from modern philosophical positions, another by inductive experience and study of the Bible itself. One position is in reality no more nor less "scientific" than the other, unless "scientific" be defined as the framework of philosophical assumptions within 'which a man to be a "scientist" must work. In that case, "scientific" refers not to the *method* of study but to the *assumptions* underlying the study; and this is the very point at issue. In some liberal quarters, especially in England, there is a growing recognition that "theology" and "history" cannot be kept separate in biblical study, but that

since Schweitzer a book written from the point of view of orthodox theology on the kingdom of God which deals comprehensively with the whole complex of problems raised by this modern liberal school.[4]

However, eschatology has been a matter of great concern to conservative Christians. In fact, it has become in recent years one of the most emphasized doctrines in the Scriptures. There has arisen a profound interest in understanding the prophetic teachings of the Bible because of the sorry plight into which the world has fallen in the last two generations. While the humanistic, naturalistic, and rationalistic philosophies have been faced by the acute problem of finding the meaning of history in a world in which the catastrophes of

---

4. The two books which contribute to this need are Geerhardus Vos, *The Teaching of Jesus Concerning the Kingdom of God and the Church* (New York: American Tract Society, 1903; reprinted by Eerdmans, 1951) ; and L. Berkhof, *The Kingdom of God* (Grand Rapids: Eerdmans, 1951). For an evaluation of the former, see below, pp. 56ff., and for the latter, p. 55.

---

the operation of the supernatural in biblical history must be admitted. This constitutes, for the historian, "The Riddle of the New Testament." (Cf. the book by this name written by Edwyn Hoskyns and Noel Davey, London: Faber and Faber, 1947; first published in 1931). The question which must be faced is the extent to which this supernatural element was operative. The thorough conservative feels that it extended to the very writing of the biblical record, and that inspiration is but the extension of the same supernatural factor which must be recognized in the person of Jesus and the rise of the Church.

We would urge that "criticism" be understood to mean the careful study of the Bible which deals with all problems by the scientific, historical method, including philology, history, exegesis, and doctrine; and the phrases "conservative criticism" and "liberal criticism" be permitted to designate the critical approach based on the assumptions of biblical orthodoxy on the one hand and of liberalism on the other. There will of course be many gradations between the two positions. While it is true that many conservatives have ignored the works of liberal critics, it must also be pointed out that liberal criticism has all too often ignored the works of conservative critics. One may search the bibliographies of many modern liberal books on the New Testament and find no mention of scholars like Theodor Zahn or J. G. Machen.

the last thirty-five years seem to be without meaning,[5] the evangelical believer has found a ground of confidence in the world-view of the Scriptures that God is indeed the Lord of history because the Son of God who lived on earth is to appear again on the earth to bring history to a victorious and glorious consummation.   If this is true, it is at once evident that the nature of the events which will attend the return of Christ is of the utmost importance.   Among those who accept this biblical teaching, several distinct positions have been maintained which involve different interpretations of the kingdom of God.

The postmillennial interpretation

Fifty years ago, it was possible to look upon the kingdom of God as a new principle, supernatural to be sure, which had been set at work in the hearts of men, which was destined to permeate like leaven all human relationships and slowly but steadily transform human society on this earth so that eventually God's will would be done among all men in all areas of life, and thus God's kingdom would come.   B. B. Warfield was sure that a golden age was ahead for the church when the Gospel of Christ had conquered the world. "The earth — the whole earth — must be won to Christ before He comes . . ."[6] "There is a 'golden age' before the Church — at least an age relatively golden gradually ripening to higher and higher glories as the Church more and more fully conquers the world and all the evil of the world" (p. 664).   This interpretation

---

5. It is profoundly significant that the effort to discover the "real Jesus" has made little progress since the turn of the century, and that the basic difficulty is not scientific but philosophical: "there is no accepted philosophy of history" (C. C. McCown, *The Search for the Real Jesus,* p. 289). Is it only a coincidence that the biblical philosophy of history was given up by the "modern emancipated man" (*lic. cit.*) just before the civilized world plunged into a series of catastrophic experiences which have rendered untenable the optimistic philosophies with which the biblical view had been displaced?

6. *Biblical Doctrines* (New York: Oxford University Press, 1929), p. 663. These words are taken from his essay, "The Millennium and the Apocalypse" which was originally published in *The Princeton Theological Review in* 1904.

has come to be known as postmillennialism, for it is held, as Warfield indicates, that Christ will not return to earth until after a golden age or millennium on earth when Christ through his Church has conquered the world. The language used by James Orr in his treatment of the kingdom leads to the same position.[7]

A more detailed defence of this postmillennial position will be found in James H. Snowden, *The Coming of the Lord: Will It Be Premillennial?*[8] The last chapter is devoted to an effort to prove that the world is getting better, and that "the kingdom of God . . . is a growth, and human history is an evolution" (p. 273). "The world's progress is a river into which every nation and every generation pours a tributary stream" (p. 274). "We have faith that nothing can stop this forward sweep of the gulf current of the ages. . . . Omnipotence is in this movement. . . . God is in his heaven, and all will yet be right with the world" (pp. 274-5). "More and more shall He whose right it is reign and the will of God be done on earth as it is in heaven. This will be the millennium" (p. 275).[9]

This interpretation of the kingdom has not sustained itself after two world wars, a world-shaking depression, and the veritable incarnation of satanic evils which the present generation is witnessing. However, an article appearing recently in a scholarly journal defending the postmillennial interpretation

---

7. Cf. above pp. 27f. It should be noted that both Warfield and Orr were critical scholars, and adherents of the orthodox theology. Cf. Warfield's *Critical Reviews* (New York: Oxford University Press, 1932) and *Christology and Criticism* (New York: Oxford University Press, 1929) for some of his best critical studies.

8. New York: Macmillan, 1919.

9. There is a notable similarity between the postmillennial position of conservative students and the optimistic evolutionary view which was developed among liberals. With the former, the kingdom began with the life and death of Christ and is extended through the preaching of the Gospel until the entire world is won for God. With the latter, there are principles at work in the world of men which will grow until a perfect society is attained. In both, the kingdom is a process of growth from small beginnings to an all-encompassing fruition.

of the Scriptures as a necessity to bolster a sound Christian optimism indicates that the position is not altogether dead.[10]

The premillennial interpretation

We have seen that the earliest interpretation of the kingdom of God was primarily an eschatological one and promised a golden age on the earth *after* the glorious return of Christ. This premillennial interpretation, as it is now called, has persisted throughout the history of the church although it has never been dominant since the second and third centuries A.D.[11] This position has been supported by many outstanding conservative critical scholars, among them Zahn, Godet, Alford, and Tregelles.[12] But none of these nor any other premillennial scholar has written a comprehensive critical study of the New Testament doctrine of the kingdom of God.

The dispensational interpretation

A little over seventy-five years ago, there arose a type of premillennialism which has exercised great influence both in England and America. Originating with the Plymouth Brethren and associated especially with the names of J. N. Darby (1800-1882)[13] and William Kelly (1821-1906),[14] this particular premillennial interpretation has been known as

---

10. Cf. Allan R. Ford, "The Second Advent in Relation to the Reign of Christ," *The Evangelical Quarterly* XXIII (1951), pp. 30-39.

11. Cf. D. H. Kromminga, *The Millennium in the Church* (Grand Rapids: Eerdmans, 1945) for a history of the millennial interpretation of the kingdom.

12. Theodor Zahn, *Introduction to the New Testament* (Edinburgh: T. and T. Clark, 1909), III, pp. 400-401; *Die Offenbarung des Johannes* (Leipzig: Deichert, 1926), II, pp. 591-604; F. Godet, *Studies on the New Testament* (New York: Hodder and Stoughton, 1873), pp. 294-398; Henry Alford, *The Greek Testament* (Boston: Lee and Shephard, 1872) IV, p. 732; S. P. Tregelles, *The First Resurrection* (London: Sovereign Grace Advent Testimony, n. d.); *The Hope of Christ's Second Coming* (London: Bagster, 1886), pp. 99, 109-110.

13. *Synopsis of the Books of the Bible* (5 vols.; London: Morrish, 1857-1867).

14. Cf. especially *Lectures on the Gospel of Matthew* (New York: Loizeaux Bros., 1943; originally published in 1868); *Lectures on the Book of Revelation* (New edition; London: Broom, 1884; originally published in 1861).

dispensationalism,[15] and has come to be exclusively identified with premillennialism in the minds of masses of American evangelicals.[16] Thousands of devout Christians know of no sort of premillennialism other than the dispensational view. The interpretation spread from England to America and has become deeply rooted in American Christian life because it received the support of some of the most godly ministers and Bible teachers America has ever known. Names like James M. Gray, A. C. Gaebelein, R. A. Torrey, A. T. Pierson, C. I. Scofield, W. B. Riley, I. M. Haldeman and H. A. Ironside have been particularly associated with this position. It is doubtful if there has been any other circle of men who have done more by their influence in preaching, teaching and writing to promote a love for Bible study, a hunger for the deeper Christian life, a passion for evangelism and zeal for missions in the history of American Christianity. They were men who walked with God. From their influence has come a host of Bible Institutes and Bible conferences which have supported the dispensational interpretation of prophecy. Probably the most influential single representative of this position has been *The Scofield Reference Bible* of which tens of thousands of copies have been sold to date, and which is now selling in increasingly large numbers.

---

15. D. H. Kromminga finds "dispensationalism," as he defines the term, antecedent to the Brethren movement, but it is not quite the same as the doctrine now under discussion (Cf. *The Millennium in the Church*, pp. 195f., 202ff.). It is not important for the present purpose to determine whether the views of Darby and Kelly were original with them or were taken over from their antecedents and made popular by them. Sources to solve this historical problem are not available to the present writer. For all practical purposes, we may consider that this movement — for dispensationalism has had such wide influence that it must be called a movement — had its source with Darby and Kelly.

16. It is not here necessary to attempt a comprehensive definition of dispensationalism. It involves many aspects of biblical interpretation, and those who may be classed as its adherents differ at numerous points. For a comprehensive statement, see Lewis Sperry Chafer, *Dispensationalism*, (Revised edition; Dallas, Texas: Dallas Seminary Press, 1951. Reprinted from *Bibliotheca Sacra* XCIII (1936), pp. 390-449). Our immediate concern with dispensationalism is only with its treatment of the kingdom of God, especially in the Gospels.

The *magnum opus* of dispensational eschatology will be found in Lewis Sperry Chafer's *Systematic Theology,*[17] where the entire range of theology is interpreted in the light of dispensational eschatology. From this work we extract the following interpretation of the kingdom of God.

Two specific realms must be considered: the kingdom of God which includes all intelligences in heaven or on earth who are willingly subject to God,[18] and the kingdom of heaven which is the manifestation of the kingdom of God at any time in its earthly form. Thus the kingdom of God appears on earth in various forms or embodiments during the centuries.

1. There was first of all the kingdom in the Old Testament theocracy in which God ruled over Israel in and through the Judges.

2. The kingdom was covenanted by God as he entered into unconditional covenant with David and gave to Israel its national hope of a permanent earthly kingdom (II Samuel 7).

3. The kingdom was predicted by the prophets as a glorious kingdom for Israel on earth when the Messianic Son of David would sit on David's throne and rule over the nation from Jerusalem.

4. The kingdom was announced by John the Baptist, Christ and the apostles. The Gospel of the Kingdom (Matt. 4:23; 9:35) and the proclamation that the kingdom of heaven was at hand (Matt. 3:2; 4:17; 10:7) consisted of a legitimate offer to Israel of the promised *earthly* Davidic kingdom, designed particularly for Israel. However, the Jewish nation rejected their King and with him the kingdom.

---

17. Dallas, Texas: Dallas Seminary Press, 1948, 8 vols. Dr. Chafer has been the President and Professor of Theology at Dallas Theological Seminary for many years.

18. Dr. Chafer does admit that the kingdom of God is a present spiritual reality in the lives of God's people (*op. cit.,* III, p. 215; IV, p. 26; V, p. 315f.; VII, p. 224; cf. also *Grace,* Philadelphia: Sunday School Times, 1922, pp. 140ff.). However, he does expressly deny that it was Jesus' purpose to establish a spiritual kingdom by his incarnation (cf. below, p. 51), and it is this question with which we are chiefly concerned.

5. Because of Israel's rejection, the kingdom was postponed until the second advent of Christ. The millennial kingdom was offered to Israel, rejected, and postponed; but it will be instituted on earth after Christ's return. Since the kingdom was postponed it is a great error to attempt, as is so commonly done, to build a kingdom on the first advent of Christ as its basis, for according to the Scriptures the kingdom which was offered to Israel was rejected and is therefore delayed, to be realized only with the second advent of Christ.

6. The kingdom, because it was rejected and postponed, entered a mystery form (Matt. 13) for the present age. This mystery form of the kingdom has to do with the church age when the kingdom of heaven is embodied in christendom. God is now ruling on the earth in so far as the parables of the mystery of the kingdom of heaven require. In this mystery phase of the kingdom good and evil mingle together and are to grow together until Christ returns.

7. The kingdom is to be re-announced by a Jewish remnant of 144,000 in final anticipation of Messiah's Return. At the beginning of the great tribulation which occurs immediately before the return of Christ, the church will be raptured, taken out of the world, to be with Christ. An election of Israel is then sealed by God to proclaim throughout all the world the Gospel of the Kingdom (Matt. 24:14) ; i.e., that the Davidic kingdom, the kingdom of heaven, is about to be set up.

8. The millennial kingdom will then be realized as Christ returns in power and glory at the conclusion of the tribulation. Then Israel, which has been gathered from its dispersion throughout the earth to her covenanted land, Palestine, will recognize the returning Christ as her Messiah, will accept him as such, and will enter the millennial kingdom as the covenanted people.[19]

---

19. Cf. Lewis Sperry Chafer, *Systematic Theology*, I, pp. 44-45; VII, pp. 223-225. There are seven stages in each of these passages but they do not coincide; we have therefore conflated them. For a more detailed description, cf. V. pp. 333-358. Dr. Chafer's work has been chosen

An almost innumerable volume of books and pamphlets has been produced by adherents of this dispensational position during the past several decades.[26] While Bible teachers differ among themselves about many of the details of the portrayal, there will be found a basic agreement on the stages of the kingdom as Dr. Chafer has traced them.

The amillennial interpretation

There has arisen in recent years a vigorous attack upon this position from several quarters by men who feel that the millennial interpretation of eschatology and of the kingdom, particularly in its dispensational form, is untenable.

Mention should be made first of Philip Mauro, who, although a layman, exercised a wide influence with his pen. Author of more than twenty-four books and many pamphlets, Mauro vigorously opposed the dispensational position.[21]

Some twenty years ago, William Masselink published a book entitled *Why Thousand Years?* or *Will the Second*

20. Influential in this literature, in addition to the Scofield Bible, have been such books as C. I. Scofield, *Rightly Dividing the Word of Truth* (Chicago Bible Institute Colportage Ass'n., n. d.) ; W. E. Blackstone, *Jesus Is Coming* (New York: Revell, 1908, frequently reprinted) ; A. C. Gaebelein, *The Harmony of the Prophetic Word* (New York: Our Hope, 1907) ; W. B. Riley, *The Evolution of the Kingdom* (New York: C. C. Cook, 1913).
21. Among his books dealing with the kingdom and eschatology are *"After This,"* or *The Church, The Kingdom, and The Glory* (New York: Revell, 1918) ; *God's Present Kingdom* (New York: Revell, 1919) ; *The Gospel of the Kingdom, with an Examination of Modern Dispensationalism* (Boston: Hamilton Bros., 1928) ; *The Hope of Israel, What Is It?* (Boston: Hamilton Bros., 1929) ; *The Church, The Churches, and The Kingdom* (Washington: The Perry Studio, 1936).

for reference here rather than other, older works because it is the most thorough and systematized. For a larger discussion by Dr. Chafer see his earlier work *The Kingdom in History and Prophecy* (Philadelphia: Sunday School Times Co., 1926). The same interpretations will be found in various notes throughout *The Scofield Reference Bible* (New York: Oxford, 1917). It should be emphasized that the sketch given above does not give a complete outline of dispensationalism but only of its interpretation of the kingdom of God.

Coming Be Pre-millennial?[22] Writing from the point of view of Covanental Theology and drawing upon the writings and instruction of Professors Vos, Warfield, Kuyper, Bavinck and Berkhof, Masselink made the mistake, so often made by amillenarians, of identifying premillennialism as such with its dispensational form. To illustrate the "whole Chiliastic scheme," he reproduced a diagram taken from W. E. B.'s *Jesus Is Coming*.[23] Although expressing sympathy for the millennial interpretation, Masselink maintained that it employs an erroneous interpretation of prophecy, denies the Covenant of Grace, repudiates Infant Baptism, has an unbiblical conception of the kingdom (which to Masselink is entirely spiritual and has nothing to do with earthly rulership), confuses Law and Grace, and gives an unscriptural pre-eminence to the Jew. Premillennialism "is a descent of ancient Judaism" (p. 20), and is quite contrary to New Testament eschatology.

Professor William H. Rutgers of Calvin Theological Seminary in Grand Rapids published his doctoral dissertation entitled *Pre-millennialism in America*[24] in which he launches as sweeping a condemnation of premillennialism as has been written. Dr. Rutgers first traces the background of premillennialism, finding its rootage in "pseudo-apocalyptic literature." He then sketches premillennialism in America, associating the doctrine of evangelical Christians with the eschatology of such sects as the Swedenborgians, Mormons, Millerites and Russellites. Rutgers then characterizes premillenarians by the categories of Judaism, exegetical nivelism, biblicism, and pessimism. He finds no value in this type of interpretation and presents an utterly unsympathetic condemnation of a movement which has "swung too far in the direction of sensual carnalistic realism" (p. 236).

Floyd E. Hamilton, formerly professor at Union Christian College in Pyengyang, Korea, in *The Basis of Millennial*

---

22. Grand Rapids: Eerdmans, 1930.
23. *Op. cit.*, p. 16.
24. Goes, Holland: Oosterbaan and Le Cointre, 1930.

Faith[25] attempts to prove that premillennialism is faced with insuperable problems in interpreting the New Testament in the light of a millennial kingdom. He insists that the amillennialist interpretation which sees the millennial kingdom as the spiritual reign of disembodied spirits in heaven with Christ during the thousand years — a symbolic designation for the period between the two advents of Christ — is the only tenable position.

Professor Oswald T. Allis, formerly of Princeton Theological Seminary and Westminster Theological Seminary, in his book *Prophecy and the Church*[26] engages in a thorough examination of the dispensational claim that the Christian church is a mystery parenthesis which interrupts the fulfillment to Israel of the kingdom prophecies of the Old Testament. Dr. Allis subjects the Scofield Bible, as the most influential representative of this position, to a searching criticism, although he quotes widely with excellent documentation from many other proponents of the position. The reader can learn much from Allis' book about the millenarian movement and the history of eschatology whether he accepts Allis' conclusions or not.

Two untechnical but thoughtful studies have come recently from ministers. George L. Murray, a Presbyterian minister in Newton, Massachusetts, in *Millennial Studies*[27] emphasizes some of the problems he finds in the dispensational position. Russell Bradley Jones, a Baptist pastor in Chattanooga, Tennessee, in *The Things Which Shall Be Hereafter*[28] attempts to prove that the New Testament provides a basic hermeneutic for a consistent and thoroughgoing spiritual interpretation of unfulfilled prophecies and that the fulfillment of the Old Testament prophecies to Israel is completely realized

25. Grand Rapids: Eerdmans, 1942.
26. Philadelphia: The Presbyterian and Reformed Pub. Co., 1945.
27. Grand Rapids: Baker Book House, 1948.
28. Nashville: Broadman Press, 1947.

in the Christian church.[29] Therefore no future restoration of Israel is to be expected nor any literal millennial reign of Christ on earth to be experienced.

The most recent volume has come from Professor Louis Berkhof, President-Emeritus of Calvin Theological Seminary, entitled *The Kingdom of God*.[30] This study is of especial interest to the present survey because its two final chapters deal with the kingdom of God as a millennial hope. In them Professor Berkhof insists that there is no biblical ground for a belief in a literal earthly millennial phase of the kingdom, and he raises five objections to the chiliastic interpretation which constitute one of the most concise and sane criticisms of the position to be found in contemporary literature because they are addressed to the basic premillennial position rather than to the special dispensational interpretation of it.[31]

Throughout these amillennial books runs a negative emphasis. Far more effort is expended in denying the premillennial view and in attacking its weaknesses than there is upon the positive position which these authors espouse. This position has come to be known as amillennialism. The kingdom of God will not involve a reign of Christ on earth for a thousand years, as Revelation 20 seems to teach, after the second

---

29. Cf. in the same vein ·Martin J. Wyngaarden, *The Future of the Kingdom in Prophecy and Fulfillment: A Study in the Scope of "Spiritualization" in Scripture* (Grand Rapids: Zondervan, 1934), and Albertus Pieters, *The Seed of Abraham* (Grand Rapids: Eerdmans, 1950).

30. Grand Rapids: Eerdmans, 1951. Although the book has just been published, it embodies the L. P. Stone lectures given at Princeton Theological Seminary in 1921-22 and unfortunately has not been brought up to date. The greater part of the book is devoted to the history of interpretation of the kingdom of God by Ritschl, the adherents of the "Social Gospel," Weiss and Schweitzer, and by the "crisis theologians" Barth and Brunner. Professor Berkhof has rendered a real service by the publication of these lectures. He analyzes with incisive criticism these several important interpretations of the kingdom. His work is well documented and is done from a conservative, critical point of view. However, the book needs to be supplemented. Many developments have taken place in the last thirty years, some of which have been sketched in the present chapter.

31. Some of the most significant of Berkhof's criticisms will be dealt with in chapters seven and eight.

advent of Christ and before the final judgment. The Old Testament prophecies which seem to envisage such an earthly kingdom are not to be interpreted literally but spiritually. They realize their fulfillment in the church, the new people of God, which has now entirely supplanted Israel as a nation so far as God's redemptive purposes are concerned. The kingdom of God is entirely a spiritual thing,[32] a present reality. The millennial reign of Christ in Revelation 20 is also to be interpreted spiritually. It may refer to the present reign of Christ in the world through the church and in the lives of God's people, a view which originated with Augustine; or it may refer to the souls of Christians who have been martyred as they now reign with Christ in heaven in the intermediate state.[33]

The best statement of the amillennial interpretation of the kingdom of God will be found in Geerhardus Vos' book, *The Teaching of Jesus Concerning the Kingdom of God and the Church.*[34] This is a helpful volume, positively written and stimulating in its judgments. Professor Vos was a critical scholar and thoroughly conservative. However, the book lacks documentation, a fact which impairs its usefulness for critical study. The treatment is too brief, failing to deal with many difficult questions. It does pay some attention to liberal critical views of its day, but it is of course out of date so far as contemporary criticism about the kingdom is concerned. Nevertheless, it is a rewarding treatment. Professor Vos takes his stand against the older evolutionary, postmillennial position and against the consistent eschatology of Weiss and Schweitzer. These were the two opposing views to be considered fifty years ago. Vos recognizes what has been almost uniformly emphasized by critical scholars since his day, that

---

32. Cf. an excellent summary of the position in O. T. Allis, *op. cit.,* pp. 69-72, where the nature of the kingdom is described as spiritual, universal and redemptive.
33. For a further discussion of this interpretation, see below pp. 142ff.
34. New York: American Tract Society, 1903; reprinted by Eerdmans in 1951.

the "reign" of God is the correct point of departure for our understanding of the kingdom (p. 27). He goes on to urge that such a reign of God must issue in a realm, a sphere of life, and that in a majority of places, the New Testament language demands the meaning of "realm" (p. 29). This realm Vos finds in the blessings of salvation and righteousness which are experienced by the church. He finally identifies the kingdom with the invisible church (p. 159) which is embodied in the visible church. Through the latter, therefore, the life and forces of the kingdom find expression (pp. 161-162). The visible church, however, is not the only outward expression of the invisible kingdom.

> Undoubtedly the kingship of God, as his recognized and applied supremacy, is intended to pervade and control the whole of human life in all its forms of existence. This the parable of the leaven plainly teaches. These various forms of human life have each their own sphere in which they work and embody themselves. There is a sphere of science, a sphere of art, a sphere of the family and of the state, a sphere of commerce and industry. Whenever one of these spheres comes under the controlling influence of the principle of the divine supremacy and glory, and this outwardly reveals itself, there we can truly say that the kingdom of God has become manifest (pp. 162-163).

Vos admits the future eschatological emphasis in the Gospels and warns against any view which completely spiritualizes the kingdom to the exclusion of the future catastrophic events which gather around the return of Christ when the kingdom will be perfected (pp. 71-72, 77). Such a warning was necessary to counteract the evolutionary interpretation which was influential at that time. The kingdom will not be perfected apart from the apocalyptic consummation when Christ returns; but this perfected stage of the kingdom is identified with the heavenly state after human history on earth is terminated. There will be no thousand year interval between the present kingdom in the church and its final perfected form.[35]

Summary

We have concluded our survey; it may now be briefly recapitulated. The Kingdom of God in the first two centuries was universally held to be eschatological and often millenarian. Origen interpreted it spiritually and Augustine identified it with the present reign of Christ in the world through his church; and thus both Origen and Augustine eliminated the millenarian interpretation. Medieval theologians identified the kingdom of God with the visible church, and the Reformers equated it with the invisible church. This interpretation of the Reformers may still be seen in contemporary scholars such as Vos and Allis who adhere to the Reformed Faith.

Under the influence of Ritschl the kingdom was viewed as a present spiritual reality in a way that was consonant with evolutionary philosophy. The activity of the Gospel in the world was interpreted in line with the movement of evolutionary progress which was destined to make the world the scene of the realization of the fullness of God's kingdom.

A reaction arose in liberal scholarship with Schweitzer and Weiss who represented Jesus as teaching that the kingdom was only eschatological and apocalyptic and that the world was immediately to come to its end when God would set up the kingdom. Most subsequent liberal studies have retained the view that the Gospels represent Jesus as teaching that the world would end apocalyptically within a generation and that at this point Jesus was in error. Critics have attempted to obviate this difficulty either by excising the apocalyptic element as unessential, irrelevant to the kernel of Jesus' true teaching, or by setting it aside as unauthentic by literary and historical

---

35. Cf. for a similar but much briefer interpretation of the kingdom L. Berkhof, *The Kingdom of God*, pp. 13-20.

criticism. Others have attempted to find some solution which would admit a present kingdom in his teachings as well as a future apocalyptic kingdom.

Recent conservative students have concerned themselves particularly about the pros and cons of the millennial interpretation of the kingdom. Premillennialism in America has been largely identified with the dispensational view, which distinguishes between the kingdom of heaven and the kingdom of God and ignores the purpose of Jesus to establish a present spiritual kingdom. A strong reaction to this type of premillennialism has arisen in amillennialism, which interprets the kingdom largely in terms of a present spiritual reality in the invisible church and denies any future millennial kingdom.

From this review of the history of interpretation, several important conclusions are to be noted. 1. Many conservative students have withdrawn from the movements of contemporary criticism and have not been concerned with the problems which have been raised by the many recent critical discussions. 2. The problem of whether the kingdom of God is both present and future has challenged both liberals and conservatives. The search still goes on to find a key which will provide an essential unity between these two aspects and which will do justice to the data of the Gospels. 3. Most conservative studies have been concerned with only one aspect of the kingdom, viz., the character of its eschatological phase, whether it will involve an earthly reign of Christ or not. Amillennialists deny the future earthly reign of Christ; premillennialists, at least of the dispensational persuasion, tend to minimize if not to deny a present spiritual kingdom inaugurated by Christ. 4. There has not been written a comprehensive study of the kingdom of God in the New Testament from a conservative, premillennial position which takes into account the critical literature; in fact, there does not exist an up-to-date conservative critical treatment of the kingdom of God from any point of view.

In these pages it is possible to deal only with four preliminary but crucial questions about the kingdom. The first and most basic question, as to whether the problems have been solved, has, we trust, been already answered in the first two chapters. There remain problems about the kingdom of God in the New Testament, especially in the Gospels. Liberal criticism has raised many questions which most conservative students have ignored. If a study is to be thorough, it must be orientated to the entire stream of modern biblical interpretation. The limitations of the present work prohibit the attempt to accomplish this task; we trust however that we have adequately demonstrated its necessity.

The third and fourth chapters will deal with the question, Is the kingdom both present and future? We shall attempt to show that the New Testament requires a view of the kingdom which involves both a present spiritual reign of Christ within the lives of God's people, and a future glorious reign on earth.

The fifth and sixth chapters will deal with the question, Was the "kingdom of heaven" postponed? Can the distinction between the kingdom of God and the kingdom of heaven as it is held by the dispensational interpretation be linguistically and exegetically sustained? We shall show that such a distinction is not essential to the premillennial position, that Jesus did not offer to the Jewish people the earthly Davidic kingdom, that nothing was really postponed, but that the kingdom which was rejected by the Jewish nation was successfully inaugurated and may be experienced even now.

The last two chapters will deal with the interpretation of Revelation twenty and will attempt to show that sound exegesis demands a future earthly millennial kingdom, and that the objections most often cited against this interpretation are not insuperable.

CHAPTER THREE

CAN THE KINGDOM BE BOTH FUTURE AND PRESENT?

Outline

The kingdom is central in Jesus' teachings
The kingdom is both present and future
The kingdom is ultimately future
The character of the future kingdom
How can the future kingdom be present?

CHAPTER III

Can the Kingdom Be Both Future and Present?

W E NOW turn to a question which has perplexed both liberal and conservative students: Can the kingdom of God be both future and present? Can it involve both a millennial reign of Christ on the earth in the future and a present spiritual reign of Christ in the hearts of his people? What is the relationship between such a future and a present kingdom?

Professor Berkhof strongly objects to a premillennial interpretation because "Premillenarians are compelled by the logic of their system to deny the present existence of the kingdom of God."[1] It must, of course, be granted that many who hold the millenarian interpretation do deny any present existence of the kingdom. This may be illustrated in the words of President Chafer, "One of the greatest errors of theologians is an attempt, as assayed now, to build a kingdom on the first advent of Christ as its basis, whereas according to the Scriptures, it will be realized only in connection with the second advent."[2] One cannot be sure from these words whether a present kingdom in any sense whatsoever is meant to be excluded, or whether the reference is only to certain interpretations which hold the kingdom to be a present entity to the exclusion of any future aspect. We must agree with Dr. Chafer that in the fullest sense of the word, the kingdom will not come until the Parousia of Christ and the establish-

1. L. Berkhof, *The Kingdom of God* (Grand Rapids: Eerdmans, 1951), p. 166.

2. *Systematic Theology* (Dallas, Texas: Dallas Seminary Press, 1948), VII, p. 224. yet cf. above, p. 50. note 18.

ment of his millennial reign; or, more accurately, it will not come until at the end of the millennium Christ turns over the kingdom to the Father (I Cor. 15:24-25). However, we believe that Professor Berkhof has overstated the case. We find no logic in the millennial interpretation which excludes a present aspect of the kingdom.

This problem must be solved not by abstract theological reasoning but by the exegesis of the Scriptures. The point of departure must always be, What do the Scriptures teach? rather than, What does logic allow? We shall turn therefore to the New Testament, particularly to the teachings of our Lord, for the answer.

The kingdom is central in Jesus' teachings

The kingdom of God was central in Jesus' message and ministry. His forerunner, John the Baptist, appeared with the message, "Repent ye; for the kingdom of heaven is at hand" (Matt. 3:2). Jesus commenced his own ministry with the same announcement, "Repent ye; for the kingdom of heaven is at hand" (Matt. 4:17). Matthew summarizes the early Galilean ministry with the words, "and Jesus went about in all Galilee, teaching in their synagogues, and preaching the gospel of the kingdom" (Matt. 4:23). Luke similarly records that at the outset of his ministry Jesus said, "I must preach the good tidings of the kingdom of God to the other cities also: for thereto was I sent" (Luke 4:43).

The Sermon on the Mount is devoted to an exposition of the character and the conduct of those who are citizens of the kingdom. It begins with a series of pronouncements of blessing to those who belong to the kingdom and concludes by making a sharp division between those who will enter the kingdom and those who will not. Jesus sent his disciples out on a preaching mission to announce that the kingdom of heaven was at hand (Matt. 10:7). At the conclusion of the Galilean ministry as Jesus was about to set out for Jerusalem, he chose seventy disciples to go before him with the message, "The kingdom of God is come nigh unto you" (Luke 10:9). In forecasting the course of the age to his disciples Jesus said, "And this gospel of the kingdom shall be preached in the whole world for a testimony unto all the nations; and then shall the end come" (Matt. 24:14). Clearly the kingdom of God was predominant in Jesus' ministry.

The kingdom is both present and future

When we analyze the temporal orientation of the kingdom in our Lord's teachings, we find some sayings which refer to the kingdom as a present reality and others which view the kingdom as though it had not yet come but was to be experienced in the future. The kingdom of God is likened to a seed which is being sown in the hearts of men, not in the future, but now (Mark 4:3ff). When Jesus said to a scribe that he was not far from the kingdom of God (Mark 12:34), he must have referred to something that was present and not far off in the future. The kingdom is like a treasure which men can find, a pearl the possession of which men can now acquire (Matt. 13:44-46).

Yet the kingdom has not yet come. It is something future into which those who have done the will of God will one day enter (Matt. 7:21). It anticipates a day in the future, apparently a day of judgment which will decide whether men shall enter the kingdom or not (Matt. 7:22-23). The twenty-fifth chapter of Matthew has to do with the kingdom of heaven which will be inherited only when the Son of Man comes in his glory to sit on his glorious throne of judgment (Matt. 25: 31, 34). "All attempts, and they have been many and ingenious, to explain these two meanings of Kingdom of God by eliminating one of them have failed."[3]

---

3. F. J. Foakes Jackson and Kirsopp Lake, *The Beginnings of Christianity* (London: Macmillan, 1920-1933), I, p. 280.

The kingdom is ultimately future

After we have recognized that the Gospels represent the kingdom as both a present and a future reality, we are faced with the problem of the underlying significance of these two aspects of the kingdom. Granted that the Scriptural data seem so to represent the kingdom, how can it be both present and future? What is the relationship between these two aspects? Which of them is primary and basic?

The answer to this last question is not to be discovered by counting the number of references to the present kingdom on the one hand and to a future kingdom on the other and rendering a decision in favor of the larger number. The answer will come only from the comprehensive study of Jesus' teaching about the kingdom. For our present purpose, we will not need to labor the point at length, for even those conservative critics who place greatest emphasis upon the kingdom as a present spiritual reality admit the essential character of the future eschatological aspect of the kingdom. We can do no better than to quote the words of Berkhof,

> Though the Lord refers to the Kingdom as a present reality, He more often speaks of it as the future state of consummate happiness, in which the whole life of man and of society will be in perfect harmony with the will of God . . . clearly the Kingdom of God is ultimately an eschatological concept.[4]

While Vos places far greater emphasis upon the kingdom as a present spiritual reality embodied in the Church, he too recognizes the full force of the eschatological future aspect of the kingdom.[5]

---

4. L. Berkhof, *The Kingdom of God* (Grand Rapids: Eerdmans, 1951, p. 18). Berkhof rightly warns against any evolutionary coming of the kingdom without a miraculous intervention of God. "The future form of the Kingdom will only be introduced by a cataclysmic change" (*Ibid.*, p. 20).

5. Geerhardus Vos, *The Teachings of Jesus Concerning the Kingdom of God and the Church* (New York: American Tract Society, 1903; reprinted by Eerdmans, 1951), pp. 41, 64-65.

The Gospel data require us to recognize the future eschatological aspect of the kingdom as the primary temporal
orientation and not as merely incidental to the present aspect.
In the Sermon on the Mount, the kingdom is repeatedly viewed
as something in the future which is yet to come. Six of the
beatitudes are cast in a futuristic setting (Matt. 5:4-9). The
fulfillment of the happiness there described looks beyond the
course of this age to a time when conditions are changed,
when grief, aggressiveness, acquisitiveness, sin, and violence
no longer dominate human society. "Only with the end of the
course of this world and the establishment of a new world
order can each grief be transformed into unmixed joy."[6]
Throughout this age, power and aggressiveness find a ready
reward, "but the promise that the meek and they alone should
be the lords of the earth, can be fulfilled only through a
complete revolution of the world, through a thoroughgoing
removal of all injustice and of all force from the world; or, in
other words, through the establishment of the all-inclusive
rule of God over the world."[7] The situation reflected in these
promises of future blessing is that of a future and final world
order, displacing the course of the present world, set up by
the mighty act of God, consisting essentially in the overthrow
of every will resisting God and every power hostile to the
good, when God alone and absolutely will rule the world as
king.[8]

While the Sermon on the Mount deals with a present
righteousness, the possession of that righteousness is viewed
as necessary not so much to live in the present world as the
necessary prerequisite for entering into the future kingdom.
Unless men have such a righteousness which exceeds that of
the Scribes and Pharisees, they *will never enter* the kingdom
(Matt. 5:20). The kingdom is not something which has

6. Theodor Zahn, *Das Evangelium des Matthäus*, (4 Aufl.; Leipzig:
Deichert, 1922), p. 192.
7. *Loc. cit.*
8. *Ibid.*, p. 194.

come, but something for whose coming men are now to prepare themselves. When it comes, it will involve judgment and a separation between men. "On that day" some will endeavor to enter the kingdom but will be excluded because they have not in this life done the will of God. Jesus himself will then be the one to whom the power of judgment is given (Matt. 7:21-22).

When a gentile centurion manifested faith in Jesus, he received the commendation that his faith would find its fullest recognition in the future kingdom. In that day, many others — gentiles like the centurion — would come from the east and the west to sit at table with Abraham, Isaac, and Jacob — Old Testament saints who apparently at that time have been raised from the dead — while the sons of the kingdom, the Jewish people to whom Jesus came and who ought to occupy those seats because of their religious heritage, will be cast into outer darkness where men will weep and gnash their teeth (Matt. 8:11-12). This again anticipates the coming of the kingdom after a day of judgment.

In the same vein, Jesus taught that those who were then his disciples would not experience the full blessing of their discipleship until the future. Because they had abandoned earthly possessions and relationships to follow Jesus, he promised them that "in the regeneration when the Son of man shall sit on the throne of his glory, ye also shall sit upon twelve thrones, judging the twelve tribes of Israel" (Matt. 19:28).

While the parables of the kingdom view it as something present, it is not present in its fullness and perfection. Evil doers will not be gathered out of the kingdom until the consummation of the age, and only then will the righteous shine forth like the sun in the kingdom of their Father (Matt. 13:38-43). The kingdom of heaven will not be perfectly realized until the division between the good and the evil at the consummation of the present age (Matt. 13:47-50).

At the last supper with the disciples as Jesus anticipated his death, he looked forward to the day when he would drink the fruit of the vine new with his disciples in his Father's kingdom (Matt. 26:29).

When Jesus came to Jerusalem for the last time, the people thought that the kingdom of God was to appear immediately. Jesus told them a parable to disabuse them of such expectations. The kingdom was to be long delayed. Jesus, who in the parable is represented by a nobleman, is to go into a "far country" to obtain his kingly authority and then to return. The coming of the kingdom must await the return of Christ (Luke 19:11-27).

Thus while there is a sense, as we shall see, in which Jesus represented the kingdom as already present, yet he continually looked forward to the coming of the kingdom in the future when the Son of Man would return in glory. The present age must run its course before the kingdom is fully manifested, before the kingdom "comes." By their acceptance or rejection of Jesus, men prepare themselves for that day when the kingdom is to come. The one group will find entrance into it, the others will be shut out. To this extent the consistent eschatology is correct: *the kingdom in its fullness is consistently future.*[9]

The character of the future kingdom

The kingdom of God as Jesus viewed it was ultimately a future blessing and would not be realized until the end of the age. What is the character of this future kingdom? Would it involve a temporary kingdom on earth? Was it to center around the reign of a Davidic King? Or was the future

---

9. Professor Vos makes the somewhat surprising statement that the "sole point in dispute" with consistent eschatology is the possibility of Jesus holding a view of the kingdom which involves a present reality resulting from his labors and extending through a following indefinite period of time. He seems to grant that "consistent eschatology," so far as it goes, is correct in its view of the future apocalyptic kingdom. *Op. cit.,* p. 41.

kingdom to be identified with the Age to Come, i.e., the eternal state, which would involve the transformation of the heaven and the earth? In other words, did Jesus anticipate a millennium or not?

Most Old Testament prophecies describe the future kingdom in terms of an earthly realm and frequently anticipate a Davidic King. Some prophecies however seem to anticipate a transformation of the heaven and the earth, i.e., the Age to Come.[10] Little careful study has been devoted to this aspect of Jesus' teachings by either conservative or liberal scholarship.[11] Even those who assume that Jesus adopted the Jewish apocalyptic eschatology current at the time have no easy solution to the problem, for there was no uniform eschatology among the Jews.[12] It is impossible to deal exhaustively at present with this question, nor is it necessary. Several facts will suffice for our present purpose.

In the first place, while the future kingdom in our Lord's teachings seems sometimes to be consonant with the Age to Come, other references picture the kingdom in terms of earthly experience. The meek shall inherit the *earth* (Matt. 5:5).

---

10. Isaiah 65:17 ff., 66:22 ff.

11. Cf. F. J. Foakes Jackson and Kirsopp Lake, *The Beginnings of Christianity*, I, p. 281.

12. The impression given by Emil Schürer (*Geschichte des jüdischen Volkes im Zeitalter Jesu Christi*, Vierte Aufl.; Leipzig: Hinrichs, 1901-1909, II, pp. 609-650; E. T. of second German ed.; *A History of the Jewish People in the Time of Jesus Christ*, New York: Scribner's, 1890, II, ii, pp. 154-183), is misleading. Three different types of eschatological expectation may be discovered. Occasionally the apocalyptic literature anticipates the kingdom as a transformation of the heaven and earth, as Isaiah 65 and 66 prophesied: cf. *Enoch* 37-71. More often, the kingdom was to be an everlasting kingdom on the earth: cf. *Psalms of Solomon* 17; *Enoch* 1-36; *Jubilees* 23. In a few places the kingdom would involve first a temporal earthly stage, to be followed by the everlasting heavenly kingdom: cf. IV *Ezra* 7, *Apoc. of Baruch* 29, 30. (Cf. the present writer's articles, "The Kingdom of God in Jewish Apocryphal Literature," the first of which appeared in the spring issue of *Bibliotheca Sacra*, CIX (1952). Many critics, like Schweitzer have assumed that because the most common view among the Jews was that of an earthly kingdom, this must have been Jesus' view. This is not necessarily true. Jesus may very well have transcended the views of his contemporaries.

The kingdom is to come and God's will be done on earth as it is in heaven. (Matt. 6:10). Many will come from the east and the west and sit down with the patriarchs who presumably have been raised to life, in the kingdom of heaven (Matt. 8:11-12), while the sons of the kingdom are to be cast out. It is doubtful if this language can be completely spiritualized. If the parable of the nobleman who went into a far country to receive kingly authority (Luke 19:11 ff.) is applied to Jesus, we conclude that he will not exercise his kingly authority until his return in the second advent, and then the scene of the exercise of his regal authority is the same place as that from which the king departed, namely the earth.

In the second place, comparative silence on this matter by our Lord cannot be construed as certain evidence that he did not anticipate an earthly kingdom. It can mean that such an earthly reign does not merit nearly so much importance as many people today attribute to it. It must be admitted that if our Gospels constituted the total corpus of Scripture, we could form no clear homogeneous concept of the future kingdom. Different aspects of it receive attention at various times. However, the argument from silence has its limitations and cannot be pressed, *unless the context requires some expression on the point in question.*[18] If the purpose of our

---

13. A study of Paul's epistles might leave one with the conclusion that Paul believed in resurrection only of the righteous, and that all who are outside of Christ would remain in their graves. As prominent as this doctrine is in Paul, nowhere does he mention the resurrection of the unrighteous, unless as some exegetes hold, the *telos* of I Corinthians 15:24 is the end of the resurrection; i. e., the resurrection of those who are not in Christ. However, it would be very dangerous to conclude that Paul did not anticipate such a resurrection. It can be deduced from his teaching on judgment, and Paul is quoted in Acts 24:15 as believing in a resurrection of the unjust. So an earthly aspect of the future kingdom can be deduced from such references as those just cited. To interpret Matt. 5:5, as does Bruce, as teaching that meekness is a "world-conquering principle" will hardly do. (Cf. A. B. Bruce in *The Expositor's Greek Testament,* Grand Rapids: Eerdmans, n. d., I, 98).

Lord's teaching required him to describe in detail the various aspects of the future eschatological kingdom but he did not do so, then we could legitimately conclude that the aspect in question was not in his mind.   If such detail is in no way required, then silence means nothing. Does our Lord's purpose in his teaching about the kingdom require such detail?   To this question, we must give a forthright No.   The kingdom of God as Jesus described it *is an absolute.*   It is, as we shall shortly see,[14] the absolute reign of a Holy God.   In the lives of men, this reign of God ultimately demands the very holiness of God (Matt. 5:48).   It demands a righteousness (Matt. 5:20) so absolute that anger is viewed as though it were murder (Matt. 5:22), and a lustful look as though it were adultery (Matt. 5:27-28).   That this absolute demand of the perfect reign of God is coupled with a realism may be seen in the provision of forgiveness (Matt. 26:28) and the extension of grace to sinners (Luke 18:13-14).   Nevertheless, the reign of God demands of its subjects and finally will make them to become what the very character of a holy God must require.   Ultimately there are no degrees of holiness, nor is righteousness relative: both are absolutes.

In the same way, the reign of God in the world anticipates the ultimate which will be perfectly realized only in the Age to Come.   The future millennial reign of Christ, which is described in Revelation 20, is to be understood as a part of his mediatorial ministry which began with his earthly ministry.   Only after his Parousia, and also after the final *telos,* which is subsequent to and not contemporaneous with the Parousia, when he has put down every enemy, will his mediatorial reign be complete so that he can turn the kingdom over to the Father (I Cor. 15:22-25).[15]   Jesus envisages this final outcome of the kingdom.   His teachings were not designed to be a textbook on the chronology of prophecy.   It was only in answer

---

14. Cf. below pp. 77ff.
15. Cf. below pp. 177ff. for a further discussion of this passage.

to specific questions of his disciples that, at the close of his ministry, he sketched the course of the age to its consummation.[16] But even then his motives were practical, and the events which his disciples were shortly to experience in the Jewish War and the fall of Jerusalem are so interwoven with the sketch of the course of the age and its termination that some students have felt that Luke 21 relates to an entirely different address than do Matthew and Mark.[17] Jesus' teachings about the kingdom have to do not with its chronology nor with all the stages of its manifestation but with *its essential character, the demands it makes upon its members, the righteousness it requires, and its ultimate perfect consummation.*

In the third place, even if there were no distinct hints of an earthly kingdom in our Lord's teaching, that fact would not exclude such a concept from the scope of biblical eschatology if some other passage of Scripture unambiguously taught such a kingdom. There is no reason why progressiveness of revelation may not operate within the corpus of the New Testament literature as well as in the Bible as a whole. It is beyond question that the book of Revelation alone in the Bible announces the duration of the kingdom; and no greater problem would be raised if it should be that the Revelation alone announces the fact of a *temporal* earthly reign, whatever its duration might be. No one insists that all of revealed truth must be found equally in all portions of the Word.

How can the future kingdom be present?

The question of how the future eschatological kingdom can also be present is by no means solved by eliminating a temporal earthly aspect of the future kingdom. If, as we have seen, the *primary* emphasis on the temporal aspect of the kingdom is

---

16. Mark 13 and parallels.
17. Cf. G. Campbell Morgan, *The Gospel According to Luke* (New York: Revell, 1931), p. 236.

upon a future eschatological blessing, the problem of how that eschatological kingdom can be also a present spiritual reality is essentially the same whether the future kingdom involves a temporal earthly reign or not. From the perspective of a present spiritual kingdom, the problem presented by a future eschatological kingdom is the same whether it includes a temporal reign on earth, or consists only of the immediate inauguration of the eternal Age to Come. Both are future; both are eschatological; both are apocalyptic. Therefore the problem of the relationship between a future eschatological kingdom and a present spiritual kingdom is basically the same for amillenarians as for premillenarians. It is, as we have seen, one of the most difficult questions with which recent liberal criticism has had to deal.[18]

_____

18. Cf. above pp. 35ff.

CHAPTER FOUR

THE SOLUTION TO THE PROBLEM OF THE FUTURE AND PRESENT KINGDOM

Outline

The meaning of BASILEIA
The kingdom is soteriological
The kingdom in the person of Christ
The kingdom as salvation
The kingdom and the millennium
Summary

CHAPTER IV

The Solution to the Problem of the Future and Present Kingdom

IN THE preceding chapter, it has been shown that the data both of the Gospels and of the rest of the New Testament require us to hold an interpretation of the kingdom of God which is a future eschatological reality and which at the same time is in some sense or other a present reality. In the history of interpretation, some scholars have emphasized the future aspect of the kingdom to the exclusion of the present aspect. In liberal criticism, the consistent eschatology of Weiss and Schweitzer and their successors has followed this course. Among conservatives, some premillennialists have denied a present kingdom while those who do not deny it so neglect it in their emphasis upon the future millennial kingdom as to make it quite unimportant. On the other hand, scholars both liberal and conservative have made the kingdom entirely a present spiritual reality, or have identified it with the Church, visible or invisible.

The meaning of BASILEIA

To deal with this crucial question we must come to the most basic question. What is meant by the "kingdom" of God? If the "kingdom" means a *single* realm over which the King reigns, then Berkhof is right in his insistence that premillennial doctrine logically excludes any present spiritual kingdom.[1] The kingdom, the domain, the realm of Christ's reign, if there

---

1. Cf. above p. 63.

is but one realm, can hardly be future and present at the same time. The millennial kingdom cannot already have come and still not have come. Many premillenarian writers operate on the assumption that this is what "kingdom" means, and Berkhof takes them on their own assumption. However, Berkhof himself would not so define the kingdom,[2] nor is that definition intrinsic to the millennial interpretation. This is a fundamental issue upon which our entire understanding of the kingdom of God rests. The basic meaning of *basileia* merits considerable attention, and the point of departure must be philological.

The primary meaning of the New Testament word for kingdom, *basileia*, is "reign" rather than "realm" or "people." A great deal of attention in recent years has been devoted by critical scholars to this subject, and there is a practically unanimous agreement that "regal power, authority" is more basic to *basileia* than "realm" or "people." "In the general linguistic usage, it is to be noted that the word *basileia*, which we usually translate by *realm, kingdom*, designates first of all the existence, the *character*, the *position* of the king. Since it concerns a king, we would best speak of his *majesty*, his *authority*."[3]

---

2. L. Berkhof, *The Kingdom of God*, (Grand Rapids: Eerdmans, 1951) p. 16.

3. "Zum allgemeinen Sprachgebrauch von *basileia* ist zu bemerken, dass das Wort, das wir meistens mit *Königreich, Reich* übersetzen, vorerst nur das *Sein*, das *Wesen*, den *Zustand des Königs* bezeichnet. Da es sich um einen König handelt, sprechen wir am besten von seiner *Würde*, seiner *Gewalt*." Karl Ludwig Schmidt, *Theologisches Wörterbuch zum Neuen Testament* (hrsg. von Gerhard Kittel; Stuttgart: Kohlhammer, 1949), I, p. 579. Cf. Further for the primacy of the abstract sense, Theodor Zahn, *Das Evangelium des Matthäus* (4 Aufl.; Leipzig und Erlangen: Deichert, 1922), p. 124ff.; Erich Klostermann, *Das Matthäusevangelium* (*Handbuch zum Neuen Testament*, hrsg. von H. Lietzmann; 2 Aufl.; Tübingen: Mohr, 1927), p. 35; Norval Geldenhuys, *Commentary on the Gospel of Luke* (Grand Rapids: Eerdmans, 1951), p. 179 and the literature cited there. Cf. also Geerhardus Vos, *The Teaching of Jesus Concerning the Kingdom of God and the Church*, pp. 26-31.

This abstract meaning is also to be found in the Aramaic word, *malkuth,* which is probably the word our Lord used in his teaching. Recent studies have confirmed the judgment of Dalman, "No doubt can be entertained that both in the Old Testament and in Jewish literature *malkuth,* when applied to God, means always the kingly rule, never the kingdom, as if it were meant to suggest the territory governed by Him."[4] Several illustrations of this abstract meaning of *basileia* are found in the New Testament. When Jesus came to Jerusalem, the people thought that the kingdom of God was to appear immediately. Jesus told them a parable of a nobleman who went into a far country to receive a *basileia* and then to return. His subjects hated him and sent an embassy to declare that they did not want him to be their ruler. When the nobleman returned, having received his *basileia,* he at once exercised this new kingly authority which he had received over his subjects by rewarding the faithful and punishing the rebellious. Here the *basileia* is clearly neither the domain nor the subjects, but the authority to rule as king in the given domain over its people (Luke 19:11-27).[5]

The same use is found in Revelation 17:12: "And the ten horns that thou sawest are ten kings, who have received no *basileia* as yet; but they receive *authority as kings,* with the beast for one hour." Clearly the *basileia* which has not yet been received is synonymous with the "authority as kings."[6] In Revelation 5:10 the *basileia* is a redeemed people; but they

---

4. Gustaf Dalman, *The Words of Jesus* (E. T., Edinburgh: T. and T. Clark, 1909), p. 94. Strack and Billerbeck define the word as "die Herrschergewalt, die Gott durch die Offenbarung seines Namens und seines Willens über seine Bekenner ausübt." (H. L. Strack, and Paul Billerbeck, *Kommentar zum Neuen Testament aus Talmud und Midrasch,* München; Beck, 1922, I, p. 172). Cf. also Paul Volz, *Die Eschatologie der jüdischen Gemeinde im neutestamentlichen Zeitalter* (2 Aufl.; Mohr: Tübingen, 1934) p. 166.

5. The Revised Standard Version translates *basileia* in this place "kingly power."

6. Again the Revised Standard Version is correct in rendering the translation of *basileia* by "royal power."

constitute the *basileia* not because they are subjects of the
king, but *because they share his regal power*: "and they reign
upon the earth." This abstract meaning may be seen also
in Revelation 17:17 and 18.

This definition of the word *basileia* must be taken as the
point of departure for the meaning of the "kingdom of God"
in the Gospels; but it will become immediately clear that the
abstract meaning by no means exhausts the content of the
phrase. It is impossible to substitute "reign" or "royal
power" or "sovereignty" for *basileia* everywhere it occurs.
The term often passes from the abstract sense to the concrete.
Ordinarily, a regal authority would involve a people, and
would find its expression in a certain realm or domain. This
normal extension of the meaning of the word is to be discovered in the New Testament both in the secular and religious
areas. Satan took Jesus up into a high mountain to tempt him
and showed him all the kingdoms of the world and their glory
(Matt. 4:8). The word here refers to distinct domains ruled
by separate kings or rulers. When Herod promised Salome
that he would give her anything she might ask, to half of his
kingdom, he spoke not of any diminution of the regal
authority he exercised but of the area over which he reigned
and all that it contained (Mark 6:23).

We have thus far limited our observations to the purely
linguistic significance of the word *basileia* and largely to its
non-religious uses. When the results thus deduced are applied
to the teaching of the "kingdom of God," we find a key which
helps us to solve many of the problems which have surrounded
this concept. If we may indicate our findings at the outset
we may say that our study of the New Testament data has led
to the conclusion that *the kingdom of God is the sovereign
rule of God, manifested in the person and work of Christ,
creating a people over whom he reigns, and issuing in a realm
or realms in which the power of his reign is realized.*

We must beware of over-simplification; but if this definition of the kingdom of God is taken as the key to the biblical teaching, it will be found that the diverse passages on the kingdom can for the most part be satisfactorily and consistently exegeted.

The kingdom is soteriological

The New Testament uniformly reflects a world view in which a restoration of God's reign is necessary. There is indeed a sense in which God is always and everywhere King. The Psalmist could say, "Jehovah Most High is terrible; He is a great King over all the earth" (Psalms 47:2). "Jehovah hath established his throne in the heavens; and his kingdom ruleth over all" (Psalms 103:19).[7]

Yet while God is the King under whose sovereign control the world of nature and men exist, there is a sense in which God's reign is not actualized in earthly history. By virtue of the Fall, mankind has turned aside from the will of God and the experience of his gracious reign. "The background of the whole picture in Old Testament is that of a world in revolt, turned aside from God, sunk, and ever sinking deeper, in unrighteousness, abandoned to idolatry and to the lusts and corruptions which are the natural fruit of apostasy from the Creator, — a world in contrariety to the divine holiness, and judged as guilty, and justly exposed to the Divine anger."[8] Against this theological background which is implicit throughout the Old Testament, the Kingdom of God is the effectual restoration of God's reign in a world which has rebelled against him. This is dramatically portrayed in Daniel 7 where the earth is ruled by a succession of four nations which are pictured as four fearful, savage beasts; but their dominion is crushed when the Ancient of Days intervenes to destroy the last beast. There appears one like unto a son of man, and to

---

7. Cf. for a good summary of the O. T. view, J. Orr, "Kingdom of God," *H. D. B.*, II, pp. 844-5.

8. *Ibid.*, p. 845.

him is given dominion and a reign that is to encompass all peoples in an everlasting kingdom. Thus the kingdom of God comes and the will of God is done among men.

In the New Testament the alienation of men from the reign of God is the constant backdrop in the drama of redemption. While God is the King of the ages (I Tim. 1:17, Rev. 15:3), that is, the sovereign ruler over all the course of human affairs and history, yet Satan is called the god of this age (II Cor. 4:4), the ruler of this world (John 12:31, 14:30, 16:11). Because men have turned from the worship of God, the world (*kosmos*) is estranged from God and lies in the power of the Evil One (I John 5:19). Since the general tenor of this age is one of rebellion to the will of God, the character of the age is described as evil (Gal. 1:4) from which men need to be delivered, and to which they should not be conformed (Rom. 12:2).

This view of a world society in rebellion against God and subservient to Satan is reflected in our Lord's temptation when Satan showed him all the kingdoms of the world in a moment of time and said to him, "To thee will I give all this authority, and the glory of them; for it hath been delivered unto me; and to whomsoever I will I give it. If thou therefore wilt worship before me, it shall all be thine" (Luke 4:6-7). Unquestionably Satan exaggerated the extent of his authority, for God is still the King of the ages and Satan cannot exercise his power apart from the permissive will of the Sovereign God. There is no Iranian or Gnostic metaphysical dualism here.[9] Nevertheless we do recognize the biblical viewpoint that Satan is exercising a very real influence in the world. So long as this state of things continues, God's will is not done by men on earth. The kingdom, when it comes, will involve the final destruction of Satan and all satanic influences.

-----

9. Cf. W. Bousset, *Die Religion des Judentums im späthellenistischen Zeitalter* (3 Aufl., hrsg. von Hugo Gressmann, Tübingen: Mohr, 1926), pp. 514-515, where such a background is sketched.

The kingdom of God is therefore primarily a soteriological concept.[10] It is God acting in power and exercising his sovereignty for the defeat of Satan and the restoration of human society to its rightful place of willing subservience to the will of God. It is not the sovereignty of God as such; God is always and everywhere the sovereign God.[11] It is the sovereignty of God in action to frustrate every enemy which would oppose God's will (I Cor. 15:25). It is not the reign of God as such; for God is ultimately reigning as the eternal King. It is the action of the sovereign God of heaven by which his reign is restored in power to those areas of his creation which he has permitted in rebellion to move outside the actual acknowledgment of his rule.[12] The kingdom of God then is God's reign, the activity of God's sovereign and kingly authority. German has a better word for it than English: *Gottesherrschaft.* "The essential meaning is not realm, but authority."[13]

It is not difficult to conceive of this abstract reign, this kingly sovereignty of God manifesting itself at various times and in various realms; and this is what the New Testament teaches. It is possible for more than one realm to embody a manifestation of God's sovereign reign in which God's regal power may be manifested in various degrees. The reiterated perspective of the New Testament, as we have seen, is the

---

10. Approaching the matter from a different angle, Schmidt, after studying the linguistic phenomena, concludes "dass Gottes *basileia* als Gottes Handeln am menschen eine soteriologische Angelegenheit ist, deren Erklärung mit der Erklärung der *Soteriologie* überhaupt in der Verkündigung Jesu Christi und seiner Apostel steht und fällt." (*Theologisches Wörterbuch*, I, p. 584).

11. G. Vos, *The Kingdom of God,* p. 30.

12. The limitations of these lectures do not permit the elaboration and application of this definition of the kingdom of God to its Old Testament setting. However, beginning with the "Protevangelium" (Gen. 3:15), the theme of redemption runs throughout the Old Testament; and the vision of God's reign in the future will see the restoration of the knowledge of God and obedience to his will restored in all the earth (Isa. 2:1-4).

13. K. L. Schmidt in *Theologisches Wörterbuch,* I, p. 582. "... die wesentliche Bedeutung nicht *Reich,* sondern *Herrschaft* ist."

eschatological ideal. God's reign will be eventually manifested in the entire creation in the Age to Come. The final form of the kingdom must include the redemption of creation itself which is now under the curse and bondage of sin (Rom. 8:20-22). The whole realm of creation will eventually become the realm in which God's reign is realized and his will perfectly done. So Christ's kingdom will be an eternal kingdom into which God's people shall enter (II Peter 1:11). It will be a heavenly kingdom (II Tim. 4:18) because God's perfect will, now realized only in heaven, will be realized in all creation. New heavens and a new earth in which dwells righteousness, i.e., in which God's will is done, will replace the present heavens and earth in which reside sin and rebellion (II Peter 3:13). There will also be a separation of moral beings. Satan will be cast into the lake of fire; all men who are not found written in the Lamb's book of life, i.e., who have not submitted themselves to the will of God, will be cast into the lake of fire, and death and Hades will also be destroyed (Rev. 20:10-15). Then God will dwell among men, and they will be his people and will serve him. Because they have submitted themselves to God's sovereign reign, they will be permitted to share it. "They shall reign forever and ever" (Rev. 22:3-5). This ultimate, perfect reign of God will be realized only in the Age to Come, after the return of Christ (Rev. 19) and after the millennial reign of Christ (Rev. 20:1-4). It is the restoration of the effectual sovereignty of God which was voluntarily but temporarily relinquished first in the rebellion of the angelic hosts and then in the sin of man.

The "history" of the kingdom of God is therefore the history of redemption, viewed from the aspect of God's sovereign and kingly power. Before the final and perfect establishment of God's reign there could be a number of mediatorial stages in which the manifestation of God's sovereignty is realized in varying degrees. God's reign may be realized less perfectly, partially, but none-the-less really in various realms during the course of this age and before the perfect fulfillment in the age to come. The character of these several mediatorial manifestations of God's kingdom can be determined only by careful exegesis of the Scriptural language. There could also be more than one realm in which God's sovereign reign is realized simultaneously. It is from such a complex that the apparently simple term "kingdom of God" has been subject to such confusion in New Testament interpretation.

Within the limits of the New Testament, there seem to be at least three realms antecedent to the coming of the ultimate glory when God's reign is perfectly realized, and for which the others are preparatory. The kingdom, the kingly power of God, was manifested in a new way among men in the person and messianic activity of Jesus. As a result of his mission, there ensued the realm of salvation in which men may now enjoy in a new way the powers and blessings of the kingdom. At his Parousia, Christ will bring a further manifestation of the kingdom during which he will continue his mediatorial ministry of subduing every enemy. Then, and only then, when every enemy is subdued will the fullness of God's kingdom be realized, and the eternal kingdom have come.

The kingdom in the person of Christ

Before the reign of God can be realized finally in the age to come, and before his reign is realized in the realm of human history during the millennium, God's reign is manifested in other areas. The language of the Gospels impels one to the conclusion that there is a sense in which the kingdom of God came to men in the person and activity of Jesus, the King. Several important passages in the Gospels teach this,[14] but they require a more detailed treatment than can now be afforded.

---

14. Cf. Matt 12:22ff., Luke 17:20 ff., Matt. 11:11ff.

One passage alone must suffice as representative of the others: Matthew 12:22-30.

One of the most frequent manifestations of power which attended the ministry of our Lord was the exorcism of demons. Wherever he went, demons were subject to his very word. He engaged in no incantations or magical ritual as Jewish exorcists of the day were accustomed to do; he but spoke a word and the demons obeyed him. It was not the exorcism of demons as such which amazed people; it was the fact that he commanded the unclean spirits *with authority* and they obeyed his mere word that gave Jesus such great fame (Mark 1:27-28).

The Pharisees accused Jesus of effecting these exorcisms by superhuman power, but by the power of Beelzebub himself, the prince of demons, and not by the power of God. Jesus replied that such a suggestion was sheer nonsense. Demonic power could not cast out demons, or else the kingdom of Satan would be destroyed by the stress of internal conflict. Satan cannot cast out Satan without destroying himself. Nevertheless, demons are being exorcised; Satan is being cast out; his kingdom is on the point of falling, for "if I by the spirit of God cast out demons, then is the kingdom of God come upon you" (Matt. 12:28). No one can enter a strong man's house to plunder his goods unless he first overpowers and binds the strong man; i. e., Jesus could not invade the domain, the kingdom of Satan, to cast out demons unless he had first bound Satan himself. There is a sense in which Satan is bound[15] and his kingdom invaded. The proof of that fact is the authority of Jesus over demons. Satan and his henchmen were helpless at Jesus' word and also at the word

---

15. It must not be inferred that this is the same binding of Satan which is described in Revelation 20:4. There Satan is bound and cast into a bottomless pit that he should no longer deceive the nations; here he is bound with reference to his power over individuals, which is indicated primarily by the helplessness of demons in the presence of Jesus and his disciples. These are not at all the same thing.

of Jesus' disciples (Luke 10:17). The reason for this was that the powers of the kingdom of God had come among men in the very person of Jesus. The kingdom of Satan had been challenged by the powers of the kingdom of God in the person of the Messiah-King and furthermore was to suffer a strategic defeat. It is this defeat of Satan by the earthly ministry of Jesus of which we read in John 12:31, "Now shall the prince of this world be cast out," and in John 16:11, "the prince of this world hath been judged." This interpretation rests upon the exegesis of the words, "But if I by the Spirit of God cast out demons, then is the kingdom of God come upon you."[16]

The meaning of this word *ephthasen* has become a bone of exegetical contention among the adherents of the several interpretations of the kingdom. The normal meaning of the word in such a context is "to have come."[17] The "consistent eschatologists" insist that it means "has come near," not "has arrived," and is evidence for their interpretation that Jesus thought the world was about to end because the apocalyptic kingdom had come near and was about to arrive. Linguistic support for this is cited from the Greek Old Testament in Daniel 4:11 where the Aramaic word, *mt'*, is translated by *phthano* in the version of Theodotion but by *eggizo* in the Septuagint. This suggests that the two words are synonymous, and that *phthano* really means *eggizo*, "to come near" rather than "to arrive."[18] According to this interpretation

---

16. *Ephthasen eph' humas.* Matt. 12:28.
17. Cf. Song of Solomon 2:12, "The time of the singing of birds is come" (*ephthake*); Daniel 6:24, "And the lions had the mastery of them, and brake all their bones in pieces before they came (*ephthasan*, Th., 6:25) to the bottom of the den"; 7:13, "there came with the clouds of heaven one like unto a son of man, and he came (*ephthasen*, Th.) even to the ancient of days"; 7:22, "the time came (*ephthasen*, Th.) that the saints possessed the kingdom." In these three passages in Daniel, *ephthasen* translates the Aramaic *mt'*.
18. Cf. J. Weiss, *Die Predigt Jesu vom Reiche Gottes* (Göttingen: Vandenhoeck & Ruprecht, 1892), pp. 12-13. The same position is taken in Wm. Michaelis, *Täufer, Jesus, Urgemeinde* (Gütersloh: Bertelsmann, 1928), pp. 73-74; E. F. Scott, *The Kingdom and the Messiah* (Edinburgh: T. and T. Clark, 1911), pp. 114-115; M. Werner, *Die Entstehung des christlichen Dogmas* (Bern & Leipzig: Haupt, 1941), pp. 51-2.

the kingdom is entirely future, it cannot be said to have come; and yet it is so near, so shortly to come, that its powers may already be felt and its force already manifested.

The "realized eschatologists" use the same linguistic data, but they reverse its significance and interpret *eggiken* to mean the same as *ephthasen*. Both words mean that the kingdom *has come*: "The 'eschatological' Kingdom of God is proclaimed as a present fact "[19] However, Dodd has been severely criticized both for his treatment of the linguistic data[20] and for the unsoundness of his basic position which eliminates any dramatic eschatology.[21]

Even though the two words may be used to translate the same Old Testament word, they need not be precisely synonymous. Essentially the same thought is expressed whether one says that a tree "reached to heaven" (*ephthasen*) or "came near to heaven" (*eggiken*) (Daniel 4:11). There is no linguistic reason for not giving *ephthasen* its proper force of "has arrived" in Matthew 12:28,[22] if we take it to mean that "the kingdom of God has just reached you" without bringing a full experience of all that the kingdom involves.[23] The problem is not alone linguistic, it is also theological. How can the kingdom of God be a future eschatological concept

---

19. C. H. Dodd, *The Parables of the Gospels* (London: Nisbet, 1936), p. 44.

20. Cf. J. B. Y. Campbell, "The Kingdom of God Has Come," *E. T.* XLVIII (1936-7), pp. 91-94; J. M. Creed, "The Kingdom of God Has Come," *E. T.* XLVIII (1936-7), pp. 184-185; Kenneth Clark, "Realized Eschatology," *J. B. L.* LIX (1940), pp. 367-383.

21. Cf. C. T. Craig, "Realized Eschatology," *J. B. L.*, LVI (1937), pp. 17-26. For further discussion cf. C. J. Cadoux, *The Historic Mission of Jesus* (New York: Harper, n. d.), p. 198, note 4.

22. Cf. G. Dalman, *The Words of Jesus* (Edinburgh: T. and T. Clark, 1909), p. 107; W. G. Kümmel, *Kirchenbegriff und Geschichtsbewusstsein in der Urgemeinde und bei Jesus* (Zürich: Niehans, 1943), pp. 54-55; also *Verheissung und Erfüllung* (Basel: H. Majer, 1945), p. 64-65; H. D. Wendland, *Die Eschatologie aes Reiches Gottes bei Jesus* (Gütersloh: Bertelsmann, 1931), pp. 48-49; cf. also H. St. John Thackeray, *A Grammar of the Old Testament in Greek* (Cambridge: University Press, 1909), I, pp. 288-289 for the word in LXX.

23. Cf. below, p. 125, note 10.

and yet be of such a character that Jesus could say that his exorcism of demons was proof that the "kingdom of God had reached to them"?

An answer may be suggested from the context of the passage. The kingdom of God has come in the sense that the powers of the future eschatological kingdom have actually entered into the scene of human history in the person of Jesus to effect a victory over the kingdom of Satan. In some sense or other, the presence of Christ binds Satan. He is no longer free to act in the way he had done previously. His kingdom has been invaded by the kingdom of God. His power over men is broken, and a new power is at work among them. While the kingdom as the realm in which God's will is perfectly done continues to be future, the kingdom as the active saving power of God has come into the world in the person and activity of Christ to redeem men from the kingdom of Satan.

Further evidence of this is seen in the impartation to the disciples of the same power to cast out demons. On two occasions, Jesus sent the disciples on extended preaching missions. The first occurred in the midst of the Galilean ministry (Mark 6:7-13, Matt. 9:35-10:42, Luke 9:1-5). Jesus had been going about through all the cities and villages of Galilee, preaching the gospel of the kingdom and healing all sorts of diseases (Matt. 9:35). The crowds became so great that he sent out his disciples to extend the scope of his ministry (Matt. 9:36-10:1). For this mission he gave them "power and authority over all demons, and to cure diseases, and he sent them forth to preach the kingdom of God, and to heal the sick" (Luke 9:1-2).[24] Each of the Gospels emphasizes the power given to the disciples over unclean spirits and demons (Matt. 10:1, Mark 6:7, Luke 9:1); in fact, Mark's

---

24. Matthew 10:7 records their ministry as an announcement that the "kingdom of heaven has come near."

account makes the exorcism of demons their most important activity.

Again, at the conclusion of the Galilean ministry as Jesus was about to journey for the last time to Jerusalem he sent out seventy disciples, once more to proclaim "The kingdom of God is come nigh unto you" (Luke 10:9). If any city rejects them, they are not to force an entrance but are to wipe the dust off their feet as a testimony against it; for in their very mission the kingdom of God has come near to that city (Luke 10:11). Terrible judgment is to befall such a city, even more fearful than that which will fall upon Tyre and Sidon, because in the very midst of Chorazin and Bethsaida acts of such great power have taken place that had the inhabitants of Tyre and Sidon beheld them they would have repented in sackcloth and ashes (Luke 10:12-13). *These manifestations of power, dynameis, were the evidence that the kingdom of God had come near.*[25] The character of these manifestations of kingdom power are illustrated by the disciples' reaction when they returned to Jesus; they reported with joy that in Jesus' name even the demons were subject to them (Luke 10:17). Then Jesus said to them, "I beheld[26] Satan fall[27] as lightning from heaven." While the disciples were engaged in preaching the kingdom and in casting out demons, Jesus was watching Satan fall from his place of power. "The power to overcome

---

25. There is a notable tendency in recent criticism to recognize that there is an element in the miracles of the Gospels which is inexplainable by "historical" study, and that the miracles are to be interpreted as signs of the power of the kingdom of God. Cf. William Manson, *Jesus the Messiah* (Philadelphia: Westminster Press, 1946), chapter III; Edwyn Hoskyns and Noel Davey, *The Riddle of the New Testament* (London: Faber and Faber, 1931), pp. 117-126; Alan Richardson, *The Miracle-Stories of the Gospels* (London: Student Christian Movement Press, 1941), chapter III.

26. Literally, "I was beholding": an imperfect tense in the Greek.

27. The rendering of the Revised Version, "fallen," over-translates the Greek aorist participle. The Revised Standard Version renders it "fall"; the aorist here is timeless and the grammar may not be pressed to refer to some event antecedent to the time of the main verb. Cf. J. H. Moulton, *A Grammar of New Testament Greek. Vol. I. Prolegomena* (Edinburgh: T. and T. Clark, 1908), p. 134.

the demons is a cause for rejoicing because it is a sign of the presence of the Kingdom of God."[28] "The fall of Satan is the beginning of the end of his kingdom. Something is achieved through the mission of Jesus and the disciples; and that which is thus begun must go on to its inevitable end in the complete subjugation of the forces of evil and the full manifestation of the sovereignty of God."[29]

It is quite wrong to understand such passages as these to mean that the kingdom of God has come in the sense that the *fullness* of the kingdom has come and that there will therefore be no future coming of the kingdom, as does C. H. Dodd.[30] The kingdom as the realm in which the will of God is everywhere perfectly done is in the New Testament consistently future. Yet there is a sense in which one may say that the kingdom of God has come in the person and mission of Christ. The kingdom has come in that the *powers* of the future kingdom have already come into history and into human experience through the supernatural ministry of the Messiah which has effected the defeat of Satan. Men may now experience the reality of the reign of God. In the future eschatological kingdom Satan will be utterly destroyed, cast into a lake of fire and brimstone (Rev. 20:10) that men may be freed from every influence of evil. However, God's people need not wait for the coming of the future kingdom to know what it means to be delivered from Satanic power. The presence of Christ on earth had for its purpose the defeat of Satan, his binding, so that God's power may be a vital reality in the experience of those who yield to God's reign by becoming the disciples of Jesus. In Christ, the kingdom, in the form of its power, has come among men.

---

28. T. W. Manson, *The Mission and Message of Jesus* (New York: E. P. Dutton, 1946), p. 550.

29. *Loc. cit.*

30. Cf. C. H. Dodd, *The Parables of the Kingdom* (London: Nisbet, 1936), pp. 123-124.

The kingdom as salvation

These manifestations of the presence of the kingdom of God have a deeper moral significance than that of mere external display. This is illustrated in the healing of the paralytic, where the physical healing of the man was accompanied by the forgiveness of his sins (Mark 2:3 ff.). The Jews were offended that Jesus claimed the right to forgive sins; but Jesus affirmed that this prerogative which was properly God's, was also his because he was the Son of Man.[31] His ministry was directed to calling sinners to repentance (Mark 2:17); he was repeatedly criticized for associating with sinners (Luke 5:30, 7:34, 15:2, 19:7); his mission was to bring men the forgiveness of their sins (Luke 7:47, Mark 2:10); he is to give his life a ransom for many (Mark 10:45). Jesus was very conscious that a new era was being inaugurated with his ministry. Luke records that at the beginning of his ministry, he read from the prophet Isaiah, "The Spirit of the Lord is upon me, because he hath anointed me to preach good tidings to the poor; he hath sent me to proclaim release to the captives, and recovering of sight to the blind, to set at liberty them that are bruised, to proclaim the acceptable year of the Lord" (Luke 4:18-19). After concluding the reading, he interpreted it with the words, "Today hath this scripture been fulfilled in your ears" (Luke 4:21). The acceptable year of the Lord has dawned; a new era has begun.

---

31. There is considerable critical discussion as to whether in the words, "The Son of man hath authority on earth to forgive sins" (Mark 2:10), Jesus used the phrase as a messianic title which he applied to himself. It has been frequently maintained that in this place the "Son of Man" is not a title, but is only a periphrasis for "man." So H. D. A. Major, *The Mission and Message of Jesus*, p. 52; T. W. Manson, *The Teaching of Jesus* (Cambridge: University Press, 1945), pp. 213-214; George Duncan, *Jesus, Son of Man* (New York: Macmillan, 1949), p. 148. In spite of the linguistic data, the force of the argument does not commend itself. The context shows that Jesus' affirmation of his right to forgive sins "upon the earth" springs from his very consciousness of being the Son of Man. Cf. N. B. Stonehouse, *The Witness of Matthew and Mark to Christ* (Philadelphia: The Presbyterian Guardian, 1944), p. 111; Vincent Taylor, *The Gospel according to St. Mark* (London: Macmillan, 1952), pp. 197f.

When John the Baptist sent from prison to inquire if Jesus really was the Messiah, Jesus replied with the words, "Go and tell John the things which ye hear and see: the blind receive their sight, and the lame walk, the lepers are cleansed, and the deaf hear, and the dead are raised up, and the poor have good tidings preached to them" (Matt. 11:4-5). Then, turning to the crowds, Jesus affirmed that John was the greatest of the prophets, but that the least in the kingdom of God was greater than John;[32] i.e., greater not in position or influence but in blessings, for the messianic blessings have now, in the person of the Messiah, come to men.

Jesus again expressed the same thought in another context: "The law and the prophets were until John; from that time the gospel of the kingdom of God is preached, and every man entereth violently into it" (Luke 16:16). A new order has come. The period of the law and the prophets is passed. John was the last of the prophets; but now that the messianic salvation has come, the least person who enters this new realm of kingdom blessing enjoys greater privileges than even John knew.

The parables about the kingdom of heaven in Matthew 13 involve a fulfillment of prophecy, for Jesus said that "many prophets and righteous men desired to see the things which ye see, and saw them not; and to hear the things which ye hear, and heard them not" (Matt. 13:17). Prophecy has been fulfilled; a new era has come.

We may admit the full force of such passages and recognize that there is a sense in which we may speak of a "realized eschatology," if we insist that the *full* realization of God's reign is still future.[33] The blessings of the future eschatological kingdom have already come to men in the experience of for-

---

32. There is a difficult problem of exegesis in this passage into the solution of which we cannot now enter. Cf. N. B. Stonehouse, *op. cit.*, p. 245 ff. for the interpretation of Matthew 11:12.
33. Cf. R. Newton Flew, *Jesus and His Church* (London: Epworth Press, 1943), p. 23.

giveness of their sins, the release from the power of Satan, in short, in the messianic salvation. The *fullness* of this salvation is not yet received, but the essence of it, the power of it, has come. In this sense one may "enter in" to the realm of blessing and salvation even though the kingdom in its perfected form is yet to be entered in the future. It was in this sense that Jesus said to Nicodemus, "Except one be born anew, he cannot see the kingdom of God. . . . Except one be born of water and the Spirit, he cannot enter into the kingdom of God" (John 3:3, 5).

Paul gives us a clear interpretation of this realm of salvation which Christ brought to men. While the kingdom of God in Paul's writings is usually a future realm, yet to be inherited (I Cor. 6:9, 15:50, Gal. 5:21, Eph. 5:5, II Tim. 4:1, 18), the kingdom is also a present blessing of "righteousness and peace and joy in the Holy Spirit" (Rom. 14:17), a realm to be enjoyed in the present life, for God has "delivered us out of the power of darkness, and translated us into the kingdom of the Son of his love" (Col. 1:13). The kingdom is future in its fullness; yet we have already been transferred into it and enjoy its blessings. While this teaching carries us further than do the Gospels, it only develops in the light of Jesus' death and resurrection what he had taught his disciples.

The kingdom and the millennium

In the Apocalypse of the things which must shortly come to pass, Jesus revealed to John on the island of Patmos that after his glorious return, there would ensue a millennial kingdom on earth (Rev. 20:1-6).[34] After his Parousia, Christ is to reign in person over human society as it is now constituted. The earth and human history will then become the realm within which God's reign will be realized to a degree beyond

---

34. We may be permitted to anticipate for the moment the conclusions we shall deduce in the final chapters, viz., that this passage of Scripture must be interpreted literally and therefore describes a temporal earthly reign of Christ before the final consummation.

anything experienced before. The powers of Satan will be curtailed with special reference to the deception of the nations (Rev. 20:3). Israel as a nation is to be saved (Rom. 11) and is to become an instrument in the hands of God for the fulfillment of the divine purposes. The prophecies of God to Israel in the Old Testament which have never been fulfilled will then come to realization. This does not mean a return to the Old Testament dispensation. The book of Hebrews makes it clear that the types and shadows of the Old Testament dispensation are forever done away as a means of access to God because of their fulfillment in Christ.

There is no retrogression in the history of revelation and of redemption. We cannot be concerned now with the details of this future reign; it must suffice to recognize that not before the millennial age when Christ rules personally over the earth will there be a measurable approximation of the will of God *on earth*. Only then will the "Golden Age" be realized; only then will every department of earthly existence — marriage, the family, the state, social life, art, literature, education[35] — be renewed and transformed. God's will is to be realized *in history*, not only beyond history; it will then be realized, however, not in a final and ultimate way, but in the continuation of the mediatorial ministry of Christ as he shall rule in person on the earth. There is nothing in the premillennial position which requires one to hold, as Rutgers charges,[36] that Christ is King only of Israel.[37] He *is* the King of Israel and Israel is to have its place in the millennial kingdom; but the millennial kingdom is not Jewish so much as it is mediatorial; "For he must reign, till he hath put all his enemies under his feet" (I Cor. 15:25). When the mediatorial ministry is completed

---

35. Cf. above pp. 27f., 46.
36. W. H. Rutgers, *Premillennialism in America* (Goes, Holland: Oosterbaan and LeCointre, 1930), p. 280.
37. Spiritually, believers have already realized the power of the kingdom of Christ (Col. 1:13).

Christ will turn over the kingdom to God the Father, that God may be all in all (I Cor. 15:24, 28).

From the perspective of our Lord's teaching about the kingdom, the future eschatological aspect seems to embrace both the ultimate kingdom and the millennial kingdom since both of them lie beyond the Parousia. Sometimes his language describing the future eschatological kingdom seems to describe the earthly millennial aspect and sometimes the ultimate, eternal aspect.[38] This should occasion no surprise, for it is but another illustration of the prophetic perspective which sees the various canvasses of future events superimposed one upon the other so that only one picture is seen. One hardly needs to be reminded of this prophetic perspective in the Old Testament which sees the two advents of Christ as though they were one. If it had been possible to gather the great prophets of the kingdom in a conference and ask them questions about the present church age, it is likely that there would have resulted more differences of opinion than now exist concerning the future millennial kingdom, for the Holy Spirit had not revealed to the Old Testament prophets the events which should transpire between the two advents of Christ. So true is this that some students are unable to find the church in the Old Testament, except in type.

Again, John the Baptist proclaimed that the kingdom of heaven was at hand, and its coming was to involve the separation of men. Some would be baptized with the Holy Spirit, others would be engulfed in the fire of divine judgment. John seems not to have understood what is now obvious that a long interval of time was to intervene between the two events which he announced. To John they were one. In view of such well known biblical phenomena, it should elicit no surprise if our Lord employs the same perspective and views the future as one great drama without making detailed distinctions between the several acts.

---

38. Cf. above, pp. 70f.

Jesus was continually concerned with two emphases in his portrayal of the eschatological drama: its ultimate accomplishment, and its immediate application. The ultimate consummation will involve the perfect realization of God's reign in all creation; and the immediate application involves the personal realization of God's reign within the lives of men by which they are prepared to enter the future kingdom.

Summary

Thus the kingdom is seen to be a single concept, the rule of God, which manifests itself in a progressive way and in more than one realm. It is *God's saving will in action.* It cannot be made an *abstract principle,* even the "principle of divine rule,"[39] for such an abstraction is too easily equated with the evolutionary optimism embodied in the magic word "progress."[40] The kingdom of God can never be divorced from the direct, personal activity of God. God's will is sovereign, yet he has permitted an apparent frustration of his will on earth by Satan, who is the ruler of this world, the god of this age. However, God has sent his Son to defeat and frustrate the kingdom of Satan. The powers of the kingdom were present in Christ. Satan was impotent before him. The powers of the kingdom entered into history in Christ to bind Satan and to plunder his kingdom. Because of Christ's life and death, men may enter into the realm of God's reign, the realm of salvation, the realm of messianic blessing and know release from Satan's power as God's reign becomes an effective power within them. Yet the fulness of these blessings and of this salvation is yet future. While men as individuals may be delivered from Satan's power, he is still the god of this

---

39. James Orr, "Kingdom of God" *H. D. B.,* II, 852.
40. Cf. William Manson, *Christ's View of the Kingdom of God* (New York: Doran, 1918), esp. pp. 18-19, for an effort to equate the teaching of Jesus about the kingdom with evolution as "controlled by and regulated by the Divine Idea."

age, and though he is defeated, the victory over him has not been consummated; he continues to exercise much of his power as the prince of the power of the air over men and nations and will continue to do so until the Parousia of Christ. Then there will ensue a glorious manifestation of God's power as Christ exercises his mediatorial rule over the world during the millennial age, during which time he will complete the subjugation of his enemies. At the end of this period, having put under his feet every enemy hostile to the will of God, he will turn over the kingdom to the Father, and then the will of God will be done perfectly and forever.

CHAPTER FIVE

WAS THE "KINGDOM OF HEAVEN" POSTPONED?

Outline

THE DISPENSATIONAL INTERPRETATION OF THE KINGDOM OF HEAVEN

DIFFICULTIES IN THE POSTPONED KINGDOM THEORY

The linguistic difficulty

The exegetical difficulty

The theological difficulty

CHAPTER V

Was the "Kingdom of Heaven" Postponed?

THE DISPENSATIONAL INTERPRETATION OF THE KINGDOM OF HEAVEN

THE PHRASE "kingdom of God" is found uniformly in the gospels of Mark, Luke and John.[1] In Matthew, the "kingdom of God" occurs but four times;[2] elsewhere, the "kingdom of heaven" (literally, the kingdom of the heavens) appears in some thirty-three places.

The occurrence of these two phrases in Matthew has been employed in the attempt to prove that Jesus offered to the Jewish nation the earthly, Davidic kingdom, which was rejected and therefore postponed until Christ comes again.[3] According to this view the kingdom of God and the kingdom of heaven are not the same. The difference is that "the kingdom of heaven is always earthly while the Kingdom of God is as wide as the universe and includes as much of earthly things as are germane to it."[4] The kingdom

---

1. The one exception is John 3:5 where the "kingdom of heaven" is found in some important textual sources as a variant reading.
2. Cf. Matthew 12:28, 19:24, 21:31, 21:43. The reading in Matthew 6:33 in the A. V. is not supported by the Greek text. The proper reading is "his kingdom."
3. Cf. above pp. 48ff., where the dispensational view is outlined.
4. Lewis Sperry Chafer, *Systematic Theology* (Dallas, Texas: Seminary Press, 1948) IV, p. 26.

In the pages that follow, we shall quote extensively from several of the most influential recent representatives of the dispensational position, in fact, so extensively that the reader may weary. This is done, however, that it may be apparent that we are setting up no straw man but that the position being discussed is widely held in certain circles and is here accurately presented.

of God is the over-all rule of God while the kingdom of heaven is the kingdom of God in its earthly manifestation, "the rule of the heavens over the earth."[5] " 'The Kingdom of heaven' . . . means the earthly kingdom promised to Israel in the Old Testament, over which the Messiah was to reign."[6] "The premillenarian distinguishes between the kingdom of God, the kingdom of heaven, and the Church. . . . By the kingdom of God chiliasts understand the all-inclusive rule of God the Father, God the Son, and God the Holy Spirit over the entire universe, particularly with regard to all moral intelligences everywhere at all time. The kingdom of heaven is the earthly sphere of the kingdom of God, and is visible and outward."[7]

It was this gospel of the kingdom of heaven which John proclaimed, and which Jesus announced as at hand, i.e., the good news that the earthly kingdom was about to be set up, if it was accepted. "In one word, the kingdom of the heavens is the *literal* fulfillment of all the prophecies and promises contained in the Old Testament. . . . *This* kingdom, the forerunner declares, now has drawn nigh, it is at hand. . . . Not only did John preach this kingdom to its Jewish, earthly form, but the Lord Himself declared that it had drawn nigh . . ."[8]

According to this view, the gospel of the kingdom which Jesus preached throughout Galilee (Matt. 4:23, 9:35) is not the announcement that God is about to bring to men a means of salvation by which they may become spiritually subjects of the King; it was rather the *bona fide* offer of the earthly Davidic kingdom to the nation Israel. "It is the Gospel of the Kingdom which he preaches. The Gospel of Grace is

5. *The Scofield Reference Bible* (New York: Oxford, 1909), p. 996. Cf. also pp. 1003, 1226; E. Schuyler English, *Studies in the Gospel According to Matthew* (New York: Revell, 1935), pp. 18, 31.

6. James M. Gray, *Christian Workers' Commentary* (New York: Revell, 1915), p. 295.

7. Charles Feinberg, *Premillennialism or Amillennialism* (Grand Rapids: Zondervan, 1936), p. 194.

8. A. C. Gaebelein, *The Gospel of Matthew* (New York: Our Hope, 1910), I, pp. 60-61.

something different."[9] Jesus proclaimed this message of the kingdom until his rejection. "By and by when His rejection by Israel is confirmed, this gospel ceases to be preached, and the gospel of grace takes its place."[10] It is Matthew's Gospel alone which records this offer of the Davidic kingdom to Israel, for it alone was written to Jewish people. "The Gospel according to Matthew is a Jewish Book."[11]

Matthew further records the rejection of the kingdom by Israel, a rejection which becomes final in the twelfth chapter. "The Lord Jesus preached the Gospel of the Kingdom from this time until its final rejection by Israel, recorded in Matthew twelve."[12] This chapter "is the great turning point in this Gospel and with it the offer of our Lord to Israel as their King, as well as the offer of the Kingdom ceases."[13] In the first twelve chapters of Matthew Jesus is concerned only with the Jews and with the offer to them of the Davidic kingdom. But when they rejected it, the offer of the kingdom was withdrawn, and the kingdom of heaven entered a new phase, its "mystery form." Jesus began in Matthew 13 to speak about the mysteries of the kingdom. By this, we are to understand "the present sphere of divine authority."[15] "The present conditions in Christendom are a mystery form of the kingdom."[16] "The kingdom now takes a form where its administration is in the hands of men while the King is absent from the kingdom."[17] "The Kingdom of heaven is now no longer that Old Testament Kingdom promised to Israel . . . [but] what we term today 'Christendom,' the sphere of Christian

---

9. A. C. Gaebelein, *op. cit.*, I, p. 64. Cf. also p. 100,
10. J. M. Gray, *op. cit.*, p. 297.
11. E. S. English, *op. cit.*, p. 16.
12. E. S. English, *op. cit.*, pp. 43-44.
13. A. C. Gaebelein, *op. cit.*, I, p. 234.
15. L. S. Chafer, *op. cit.*, V, p. 350.
16. *Ibid.*, VII, p. 224.
17. Chas. Feinberg, *op. cit.*, p. 95.

profession."[18] "It includes the whole sphere of Christian profession saved and unsaved, so-called Romanists and Protestants, all who are naming the name of Christ."[19] "It may be real or not, but every professing Christian is in the kingdom of heaven. Every person who, even in an external rite, confesses Christ, is not a mere Jew or Gentile, but in the kingdom. It is a very different thing from a man's being born again and being baptized by the Holy Ghost into the body of Christ. Whoso bears the name of Christ belongs to the kingdom of heaven. It may be that he is only a tare there, but still there he is."[20]

This understanding of the kingdom of heaven has its most important consequences in the interpretation of the Sermon on the Mount in Matthew 5-7. While this sermon has a "beautiful moral application to the Christian," its literal and primary application is to be to the future earthly kingdom and not to Christian life. "In this sense it gives the divine constitution for the righteous government of the earth. . . . The Sermon on the Mount in its primary application gives neither the privilege nor the duty of the Church. These are found in the Epistles. Under the law of the kingdom, for example, no one may hope for forgiveness who has not first forgiven. Under grace the Christian is exhorted to forgive because he is already forgiven."[21] "Had the Holy Spirit meant the application to be for the Church, He would have brought the discourse to our attention after the Lord first mentioned the Church, in Matthew sixteen. Church doctrine is revealed in the Epistles. The Christian has a heavenly calling; 'The Sermon on the Mount' is to a great extent

---

18. A. C. Gaebelein, *The Annotated Bible. The New Testament* (New York: Our Hope, 1913), I, pp. 33, 34. Cf. also E. S. English, *op. cit.,* p. 91; James M. Gray, *op. cit.,* p. 302.
19. A. C. Gaebelein, *The Gospel of Matthew,* I, pp. 263-264.
20. William Kelly, *Lectures on the Gospel of Matthew* (New York: Loizeaux Brothers, 1943; first printed in 1868), p. 266.
21. *The Scofield Reference Bible,* pp. 999-1000.

earthly in its application."[22] "It tells us not how to be acceptable to God, but it does reveal those who will be pleasing to God in the kingdom. . . . The Sermon on the Mount is legal in its character; it is the law of Moses raised to its highest power."[23] "All the kingdom promises to the individual are based on human merit. . . . It is a covenant of works only and the emphatic word is *do*. . . . As the individual forgives, so will he be forgiven. And except personal righteousness shall exceed the righteousness of the scribes and Pharisees, there shall be no entrance into the kingdom of heaven. To interpret this righteousness which is required to be the imputed righteousness of God, is to disregard the teaching of the context, and to introduce an element which is not found in the whole system of divine government."[24] "As a rule of life, it is addressed to the Jew before the cross and to the Jew in the coming kingdom, and is therefore not now in effect."[25] "This discourse is no more related to the Church than the Messianic, Davidic, earthly kingdom is related to the Church, and those who apply it to the Church seem little aware of the problems which are involved."[26] "All of these legal utterances of Christ's were in full divine force when they were spoken, but the child of God of this age has been saved from the entire merit system."[27] "How far removed is a mere man-wrought righteousness which exceeds the righteousness of the scribes and the Pharisees from the 'gift of righteousness' bestowed on those who receive 'abundance of grace'."[28] Yet many "embrace a system demanding supermerit requirements and seem not to recognize that the priceless things per-

---

22. E. S. English, *op. cit.*, p. 46.
23. Charles Feinberg, *op. cit.*, p. 90.
24. L. S. Chafer, *Systematic Theology*, IV, pp. 211-212.
25. *Ibid.*, V, p. 97.
26. *Ibid.*, p. 102.
27. *Ibid.*, p. 105.
28. *Ibid.*, p. 112.

taining to both a perfect standing and eternal security in Christ are omitted."[29]

"The 'Sermon on the Mount' does not set forth the terms of salvation for sinners. . . . but is primarily Jewish and pertains to conditions on the earth when the manifested Kingdom of the Messiah is in vogue."[30]

DIFFICULTIES IN THE POSTPONED KINGDOM THEORY

It is immediately obvious that a system which takes this greatest portion of Jesus' teaching away from the Christian in its direct application must receive a penetrating scrutiny. This is the reason the dispensational interpretation of the kingdom concerns us so vitally. When Christians will not use the Lord's Prayer because it is given for the kingdom age and not for the present age, we must test carefully the validity of the position. These are not unimportant peripheral matters, but the heart of the teachings of our Lord.

We have seen that the position is maintained on the basis of the distinction between the kingdom of God and the kingdom of heaven. We must now ask, What is the reason for and the validity of this distinction? Why should we distinguish thus between the two phrases? What is there in the Scripture to suggest that the kingdom of God refers to God's over-all universal rule while the kingdom of heaven refers to the application of this rule to the earth?

The problem really resolves itself into two parts, which may be indicated as questions. First, does the kingdom of heaven refer to the earthly Davidic kingdom as over against the more comprehensive term, the kingdom of God? Second, did Jesus actually offer to the Jews the earthly and Davidic kingdom? As the subject is treated by American dispensationalists, these two questions are one and the same; but they are not necessarily so. For instance, George N. H. Peters,

---

29. *Loc. cit.*
30. James M. Gray, *op. cit.*, p. 297.

in his enormous three volume work of 2175 pages, recognizes an identity of meaning in these two expressions but holds that both refer to the Davidic kingdom prophesied in the Old Testament which Jesus offered Israel and which was by them rejected.[31] Would anyone coming to the Gospels for the first time to study these two phrases discover such a distinction?

The linguistic difficulty

We shall deal first with the linguistic problem. It is to be noted at the outset that the two expressions seem to be quite interchangeable in the Gospels. There is no need in support of this statement to present a complete list of the uses of the two expressions; but no student who is investigating this question can be satisfied until he has done this and surveyed the evidence for himself. A few illustrations must suffice. In Matthew, Jesus begins his ministry with the announcement that the kingdom of heaven is near (Matt. 4:17), but in Mark he announces that the kingdom of God has come near and men are to repent and believe in the Gospel (Mark 1:15). In Matthew, the twelve offer the kingdom of heaven to Israel (Matt. 10:6-7), but in Luke they offer the kingdom of God (Luke 9:2). If in Matthew the Sermon on the Mount announced as the law of the kingdom of heaven is the law of the future earthly kingdom (Matt. 5:3), in Luke it is announced as something else, the law of the kingdom of God (Luke 6:20). According to Matthew the parables portray the mystery of the kingdom of heaven (Matt. 13:11), but in Mark (4:11) and in Luke (8:10) it is the kingdom of God. If in Matthew a

---

31. George N. H. Peters, *The Theocratic Kingdom of Our Lord Jesus, the Christ* (New York: Funk and Wagnalls, 1884), I, p. 283ff. Peters goes on to say that the rejected kingdom was taken from the Jews (p. 389), is postponed (p. 590) until the close of the tribulation (p. 419) and is to be given to another nation whom God is now calling out (p. 412), who thereby become heirs of Adam (p. 587). The new election does not remove the election of the Jewish nation as a nation (pp. 416-7), which is yet to be restored to the favor of God.

Jewish remnant is to announce at the end of the age the good news that the earthly kingdom, the kingdom of heaven, is about to be set up (Matt. 24:14), then Mark says something quite different — that the *gospel* must be preached first to all the nations (Mark 13:10).

Furthermore, if such a distinction is to be made, no adequate explanation has been suggested for the four times the expression "kingdom of God" occurs in Matthew. One illustration will suffice. After the conversation with the rich young ruler, Jesus said to His disciples, "Verily, I say unto you, it is hard for a rich man to enter into the kingdom of heaven. And again I say unto you, It is easier for a camel to go through a needle's eye, than for a rich man to enter into the kingdom of God" (Matt. 19:23-24). Here the two terms are clearly synonymous, and both are equivalent to salvation, eternal life; for the disciples immediately ask, "Who then can be saved?" Jesus replied, "With men this is impossible, but with God all things are possible." The meaning is that it does not lie within the scope of human effort or attainment to be saved; salvation is a miracle which can be wrought only by God. The force of the miracle is especially notable in the case of a rich man. Salvation involves the complete surrender to God, and a rich man has so much more to give up than a poor man that the necessity of the miraculous work of God is much more evident. It is true that the kingdom of heaven is here mentioned as something future; but so is eternal life. While in one sense eternal life becomes a present possession of the believer, at the same time its full realization is future, to be received only after Christ returns.[32]

---

32. Even in the Gospel of John where the present possession of eternal life is most frequently emphasized (cf. 3:15, 3:36, 5:24-26, etc.), it has also a future realization. The recipient of it still dies, but he will be raised up at the last day in the "resurrection of life" (5:29). "He who loveth his life loseth it; and he that hateth his life in this world shall keep it unto life eternal" (12:25). From one point of view, eternal life and membership in the kingdom of God are two ways of expressing the same thing. (Cf. J. H. Bernard, *A Critical and Exegetical Commentary on the Gospel According*

The exegetical difficulty

Not only is it difficult to explain adequately the linguistic phenomena by this aspect of the dispensational teaching, but a number of passages present acute exegetical difficulties. The first is found in the passage we have just discussed. Jesus said that it is hard for a rich man to enter the kingdom of heaven (Matt. 19:23). According to the dispensational theory, the kingdom of heaven through Matthew 12 is the earthly Davidic kingdom; but beginning with Matthew 13, the offer of the earthly kingdom is withdrawn and the kingdom of heaven enters its "mystery form," professing Christianity, Christendom. This interpretation cannot possibly be sustained in this passage. As a matter of fact, it is not difficult for a rich man to enter a professing Christian church and to take upon himself the Christian profession. The nominal church is usually quite ready to welcome a rich man into its membership. If there is any truth in this dispensational distinction, it must be drastically modified at this point,[33] and such a modification destroys the consistency of the position.

The same difficulty is to be found in interpreting the kingdom of heaven in Matthew 18:3-4. The disciples ask Jesus, "Who is greatest in the kingdom of heaven?" Placing a child in their midst he said, "Except ye turn and become as little children, ye shall in no wise enter into the kingdom of heaven. Whosoever therefore shall humble himself as this little child, the same is the greatest in the kingdom of heaven." It is

---

33. The authors heretofore mentioned do not face this difficulty or attempt to solve the problem raised by this apparent contradiction in their interpretation of the kingdom of heaven. Cf. E. S. English, *op. cit.*, pp. 137-138; A. C. Gaebelein, *The Gospel of Matthew*, II, p. 106. Gaebelein interprets this passage as though the phrase "kingdom of heaven" did not occur here at all. There is no reference to this passage in the *Index* of Dr. Chafer's *Systematic Theology.*

---

to *St. John*, New York: Scribner's, 1929, I, p. clx-clxi; C. J. Wright, *The Eternal Kingdom*, London: James Clarke, n. d., p. 19). This fact does not as we have seen (cf. Chapter II), exclude a future literal earthly aspect of the kingdom of God before the final consummation.

obvious that the kingdom of heaven here is not Christendom but is the precise equivalent of the kingdom of God, God's true reign, salvation. Dispensational treatments recognize this. "What the Lord tells His disciples here is practically the same which Nicodemus heard from His lips in that night visit. The kingdom must be entered in and that means conversion by being born again."[34] "To enter into the Kingdom of the heavens, to enjoy eternal life with God the Father and God the Son, one *must* be converted, *turned about*; one must be *born again*."[35] None of these interpreters deal with the problem which this passage raises for the dispensational understanding of the kingdom of heaven. They fail to show how the kingdom of heaven can be at the same time Christendom — the kingdom in mystery form as the theory requires — and the true realm of salvation as this passage requires.

We are forced to conclude that no study of the two phrases within the Gospels would suggest the distinction so often made, nor, in fact, can it be sustained by exegesis. There are problems standing in the way of any effort consistently to interpret the kingdom of heaven as indicating in Matthew 1-12 the earthly Davidic kingdom and after Matthew 13 the kingdom

---

34. A. C. Gaebelein, *op. cit.*, II, p. 80. Gaebelein has not consistently applied the dispensational meaning of the "kingdom of heaven" to the Sermon on the Mount. He says that the Sermon is primarily for "the millennial earth and the Kingdom to come" (I, p. 110). Yet it also has an application to the believer in this age. He thus interprets the "higher righteousness" demanded for entrance into the kingdom as that which is found only in the saved man, who knows the righteousness of Romans 3:21-26, the righteousness of Christ (I, p. 123-124); but he interprets the Lord's Prayer as designed neither for the future kingdom, nor for the Christian, but for the disciples to use until Pentecost (I, p. 140). Christians cannot pray "thy kingdom come," for "as believers we do not wait for the coming of the King and the establishment of the kingdom in the earth, but we wait for the coming of the Lord to take us out of the earth" (I, p. 143). The petition "forgive us . . . as we forgive" is passed over in a footnote because it "is a legal, an Old Testament petition" (*loc. cit.*). This illustrates the problems which the dispensational interpretation of the kingdom of heaven raises.

35. E. S. English, *op. cit.*, p. 123. Italics his. Again Dr. Chafer has no reference to this verse in his *Systematic Theology*.

in "mystery form," Christendom, which require such a stretching of the theory as to cause it to break.[36]

It is not enough to say that since the two have almost all things in common, we are to expect the interchange of expression which is found in the Gospels.[37] If the kingdom of God in "mystery form" is Christendom, then it does not have almost all things in common with the true kingdom of God. It is difficult to see how false doctrine, if this is what leaven means,[38] can be predicated of the true kingdom of God as it must be since Luke's account of the parables describes the kingdom of God by the parable of the leaven (Luke 13:21). Christendom may become infused with corruption and evil doctrine, but not the true kingdom of God. The kingdom of God is "righteousness and peace and joy in the Holy Spirit" (Rom. 14:17).

The theological difficulty

There remains the greatest difficulty of all, the theological difficulty, which involves the whole question of whether or not Jesus actually offered to Israel the earthly Davidic kingdom. It should now be clear that the phrase, the kingdom of heaven, does not derive this connotation of the earthly kingdom from its use in the Gospels. Where then are we to look for this meaning?

Although it is not usually clearly stated, this distinction is to be deduced from the Old Testament background. The

36. This difficulty is illustrated by Dr. Thiessen's statement that the kingdom of heaven means 1) the millennial kingdom yet to come which was promised to David; 2) the mixed conditions now known as Christendom; and 3) the "spiritual kingdom, the same as the kingdom of God (without any implications of an earthly kingdom)." (H. C. Thiessen, *Introductory Lectures in Systematic Theology*, Grand Rapids: Eerdmans, 1949, p. 406). This seems tantamount to an admission that it is synonymous with the kingdom of God.

37. *The Scofield Reference Bible*, p. 1003.

38. L. S. Chafer, *op. cit.*, VII, p. 225; *The Scofield Reference Bible*, p. 1016; A. C. Gaebelein, *op. cit.*, I, pp. 287-293; E. S. English, *op. cit.*, I, pp. 99-100.

kingdom of heaven occurs only in Matthew. Matthew, it is affirmed, is the Jewish gospel, written to the Jewish people; therefore the kingdom of heaven must have reference to the kingdom which the Jews in particular expected, the kingdom prophesied in the Old Testament, the earthly Davidic kingdom. Dr. Feinberg affirms: "There is no explanation offered as to the meaning of the 'kingdom' in his (John's) message, for the people knew what was implied by his words. . . . There was no need to describe the conditions and characteristics of the kingdom, for that had been done so repeatedly and minutely. Nor was it necessary to inform them that the kingdom could not and would not be established without the rightful King."[39] "Nor does Christ explain what is meant by these words; His hearers knew full well their import. How unwarranted is the assertion, then, of those who find that Christ's ideas and conceptions of the kingdom involved something far removed from the thought of His hearers."[40]

The force of this reasoning must be felt whether or not a distinction is made between the kingdom of God and the kingdom of heaven. One can urge the full force of this logic, as does Peters,[41] and find no difference between the two phrases. It is true that Jesus never defined what he meant by kingdom of God or kingdom of heaven, and we can only assume that the announcement that the kingdom of God was near was full of meaning to his hearers. There is no evidence that they reacted with any measure of surprise to the announcement of either John or Jesus. The Old Testament frequently promised the coming of a time when the kingdom would be restored to Israel; and it is undoubtedly true that this is the meaning which the Jews attributed to Jesus' proclamation. We may be confident of this, because after the multiplying of the five loaves and the two fishes so that five thousand were fed, the

---

39. Charles Feinberg, *op. cit.*, p. 87.
40. *Ibid.*, p. 89.
41. Cf. above, p. 107, footnote 31.

people were prepared to take Jesus and force him to become their king (John 6:15). What a wonderful thing to have a king who could equip the crowds with arms as he had just provided the multitude with food. Here was an arsenal that could promise victory over Rome.

Are we to conclude that because the Jews interpreted the "kingdom of God" as the Davidic kingdom that Jesus' announcement that the kingdom of heaven was at hand meant that he was prepared to inaugurate the promised earthly Davidic kingdom of Israel, if Israel would accept him, their Messiah? So it has been affirmed. "No other kingdom message could have thus been received by Jewish people in that day."[42]

On the answer to this question rests the so-called "postponed kingdom" theory. This theory has been vigorously espoused because of the effort on the part of non-millenarians to interpret the kingdom *entirely* as a present spiritual reality, without any future earthly manifestation. However, such a theory is not necessary and it is beset by grave difficulties. It is very possible that our Lord offered the Jewish people something which they misunderstood and misinterpreted. In fact, their very misunderstanding may well have been the very reason why they did not accept him. He did not offer them the sort of kingdom they wanted. Had he offered them the earthly, Davidic kingdom, they would have accepted it; but that was not yet to be. Before the coming of the earthly phase of the kingdom, there must come another manifestation of the kingdom, in *saving* power. The cross must precede the crown.

The clue to this interpretation is found in this fact: Jesus did not offer to the Jews the earthly kingdom *any more than he offered himself to them as their glorious, earthly King.* Here we may take our stand on firm ground. It has been affirmed that ". . . Israel had never dreamed of a kingdom

---

42. L. S. Chafer, *op. cit.,* V, p. 343.

apart from the presence and power of the expected King."[43] However, Jesus did not present himself to Israel as the Davidic king, *as Israel interpreted that kingship.* He was the King, indeed. Matthew makes this as clear as can be. But he came not on a throne of glory, but "meek, riding upon an ass" (Zech. 9:9). "This explicit prediction as to the manner of Christ's offer of Himself as Israel's King at His first advent, is not to be confused with His resistless coming as their Messiah in power and great glory at His second advent."[44] This is precisely the key to the solution of the problem. The coming of the Messiah was to be twofold. He was to come in meekness, in humility, to suffer and die; he was also to come in power and glory to judge and to reign. In the same way, God's kingdom was first to come to men in a spiritual sense, as the Saviour-King comes in meekness to suffer and die, defeating Satan and bringing into the sphere of God's kingdom a host of people who are redeemed from the kingdom of Satan and of sin; and subsequently it is to be manifested in power and glory as the King returns to judge and reign.

We are under no more obligation to interpret Jesus' offer of the kingdom in light of the Jew's understanding of it than we are to interpret his messiahship in light of Jewish interpretation. It is the inspired record, not Jewish theology, that is our guide. The Jews were not looking for a suffering Messiah. The cross was an offence to the Jews (I Cor. 1:23). Although the disciples had become convinced that Jesus was the Messiah, when Jesus told them that he was to die, they

---

43. L. S. Chafer, *op. cit.,* V. p. 343. It is a matter of fact that the apocalyptic literature not infrequently portrays the coming of the kingdom without any mention of a king or Messiah. There is no Messiah, apart from God himself, in the *Sibylline Oracles, Jubilees, Assumption of Moses,* or *Enoch* 1-37, although in each of these works the kingdom is eagerly expected and vividly portrayed. In *Jubilees* the power of the Law alone is sufficient to usher in the kingdom. Cf. the present author's series "The Kingdom of God in Jewish Apocryphal Literature" beginning in the spring issue of *Bibliotheca Sacra,* CIX (1952).

44. L. S. Chafer, *op. cit.,* I, p. 45.

could not understand it. Peter even dared to rebuke him saying, "God forbid, Lord! This shall never happen to you" (Matt. 16:22). The Messiah is not to die, he is to reign! He is not to suffer, he is to deliver the suffering. He is not to go to the cross, he is to sit upon a throne. Again and again Jesus reiterated that he was to die, but the disciples never understood what he meant; and when he finally was seized and led away, a prisoner, they scattered and fled. After his death they were crushed with despair. "We *had* hoped that he was the one to redeem Israel" (Luke 24:21 RSV), but hope fled with his death. The disciples did not understand the meaning of Jesus' death until he interpreted it to them after his resurrection (Luke 24:27).

Today, one may well ask how the Jews missed the clear Old Testament prophecies that Messiah was to suffer as well as to reign. The Old Testament points clearly to this fact. The fifty-third chapter of Isaiah predicts it; the twenty-second Psalm describes it. After the passion had taken place the disciples were able to see in the Old Testament prophecies things which they had never before understood. The experience on the Emmaus Road when Jesus began with Moses and all the prophets to interpret in all the Scriptures the things concerning himself was utterly novel to the disciples. They had never heard of such things. They had read the Scriptures, but they had not applied them to the Messiah. It is to us a revealing fact that in the whole range of Jewish apocryphal literature where there occur various concepts of the expected Messiah and kingdom, there never once appears a Messiah who, in fulfillment of Isaiah 53, was to die for the sins of his people.[45]

---

45. In IV *Esra* 7:27-31 alone there appears a *dying* Messiah. "For my Son the Messiah shall be revealed, together with those who are with him, and shall rejoice the survivors four hundred years. And it shall be, after these years, that my Son the Messiah shall die, and all in whom there is human breath. Then shall the world be turned into the primaeval silence seven days, like as at the first beginnings; so that no man is left. And it shall be after seven days that the Age which is not yet awake shall be roused, and that which is corruptible shall perish . . . And the Most High

The Messiah was always to reign, never to die. Against this uniform interpretation of the Old Testament we are to understand the New Testament portrayal of the self-disclosure of Jesus. The disciples shared some of the beliefs which are found in the apocryphal literature, for similar expectations are reflected in various utterances of theirs in the Gospels. The kingdom was to be restored to Israel, and the disciples expected thrones at the side of Jesus to share his regal authority. Even John the Baptist was perplexed when Jesus did not act like such a Messiah. Judgment did not ensue; there was no apocalyptic separation between the good and the bad. From his prison John sent to Jesus to ask if he were in fact the Messiah, or if John had been wrong in his announcement and another was to be expected (Matt. 11:2-6). For the disciples, the period of training during the days of his flesh was a time of learning that Jesus was in very fact the Messiah even though he did not fill the role expected of him. They had to come to a new understanding of what the messianic mission was to involve.

In the same way, we are to interpret the message of the kingdom. The kingdom, the rule of God, is indeed to have a glorious manifestation when Christ, as the glorious King, rules over the earth in fulfillment of the Old Testament prophecies. But before that manifestation of God's rule there must intervene another revelation of God's regal power in a spiritual realm as the King comes among men in humility to inaugurate a new reign of God in the hearts of men. This is not to deny the future millennial rule; to do so is to do injustice to other passages of Scripture. To insist that the spiritual reign of Christ, the present inner aspect of God's kingdom, is the entirety of the kingdom and thereby to deny a future glorious

---

shall be revealed upon the throne of judgment." Here we have a dying Messiah, but he dies at the termination of the temporal earthly kingdom, which is here of four hundred years duration, and his death avails nothing and is of no purpose. This is one of the most curious passages in the apocryphal literature.

manifestation, is to make as one-sided an emphasis as to insist that the kingdom is nothing but a future earthly reign of Christ and has no present spiritual reality. Both the present and the future are included in the fullness of the revelation of God's kingly power.[46]

It is difficult to see how Jesus could have offered to Israel the earthly Davidic kingdom *without the glorious Davidic King* who was to reign in that kingdom. The very fact that he did not come as the glorious King, but as the humble Savior, should be adequate evidence by itself to prove that his offer of the kingdom was not the outward, earthly kingdom, but one which corresponded to the form in which the King himself came to men.

---

46. The difficulty of bringing the disciples to an understanding of the true nature of the kingdom in the present age and its relationship to the future kingdom is further illustrated by Acts 1:6. Even after the Resurrection, the disciples still failed to understand that it was not God's purpose to inaugurate the glorious phase of the kingdom without the glorious appearing of Christ. Even as they did not realize that it was God's purpose for the Messiah to suffer and die before he should come in glory (Luke 24:26), so they failed to appreciate that the kingdom was to come in a spiritual realm before it should be established with visible glory. It was not for them to know the times and seasons of the appearing of the glorious phase of the kingdom. God's hour for the earthly kingdom was not yet. For the present, they must bear witness to the death and resurrection of Christ in all the world. In God's own time, the kingdom would come in glory.

CHAPTER SIX

THE LINGUISTIC INTERPRETATION OF
THE "KINGDOM OF HEAVEN"

Outline

The background of "kingdom of heaven"
The meaning of "kingdom of heaven"
The kingdom which Jesus preached
The kingdom and the Sermon on the Mount
The kingdom and the parables
Summary

CHAPTER VI

The Linguistic Interpretation of the
"Kingdom of Heaven"

IT IS time now for us to turn to a positive statement of the
matter. The occurrence of the two expressions, the kingdom of God and the kingdom of heaven, may be satisfactorily
explained without resorting to the effort to find a difference
in meaning.

The background of "kingdom of heaven"

Neither phrase seems to have become a set idiom before
New Testament times. The "kingdom of heaven" does not
appear anywhere in Jewish-Greek writings before it is found
in Matthew's Gospel.[1] However, the equivalent phrase is
found in the talmudic literature quite frequently: *malkuth*
shamayim.[2] This literature cannot be taken as antecedent to
the time of our Lord's ministry even though some old tradi-
tions may be preserved in it. It does reflect the fact that during the succeeding centuries, the phrase became deeply imbed-
ded in Jewish idiom.

---

1. One is surprised to read from the pen of H. D. A. Major, that it is "a
phrase derived from Jewish apocalypses." (*The Mission and Message of
Jesus*, New York: Dutton, 1938, p. 35). The thought may be found, but
the phrase itself does not appear in pre-Christian writings. It is found in
III *Baruch* 11:2 (cf. R. H. Charles, ed.; *The Apocrypha and Pseudepigrapha*, II, p. 539), but this book is not usually dated before the second century A.D. (cf. R. H. Charles, *op. cit.*, p. 530; H. H. Rowley, *The Relevance
of Apocalyptic*, London, Lutterworth, 1947, p. 96).

2. Cf. H. L. Strack and Paul Billerbeck, *Kommentar zum Neuen Testament aus Talmud und Midrasch* (München: Beck, 1922), I, pp. 172-180.

The phrase, the kingdom of God, occurs infrequently in the Jewish literature known to antedate the New Testament.[3] The concept of the kingdom constantly recurs, but the idiom itself rarely is found. The two phrases seem to have become common idioms only in New Testament times and perhaps through the medium of Jesus' teachings. The nearest to the exact phrase is found in *Psalms of Solomon* 17:4, "The kingdom of our God is forever over the nations in judgment"; *Wisdom of Solomon* 10:10, "She (wisdom) showed him God's kingdom, and gave him knowledge of holy things."

The meaning of "kingdom of heaven"

Practically all modern critical scholarship recognizes that the difference between the two phrases is one of language only.[4] The native tongue of the Jews was Aramaic, and our Lord employed this language in his ministry. His sayings in our Gospels are translations into Greek from the Aramaic.[5] It is a commonplace that the reverence of the Jewish people for God led them to avoid the use of the divine name as much as possible and to substitute other expressions. One of the

---

3. Cf. Gustaf Dalman, *The Words of Jesus* (E. T., Edinburgh: T. and T. Clark, 1909), pp. 91-94; Paul Volz, *Die Eschatologie der jüdischen Gemeinde im neutestamentlischen Zeitalter* (Zweite Aufl.; Tübingen: Mohr, 1934), pp. 165-167; W. Bousset, *Die Religion des Judentums im späthellenistischen Zeitalter* (Dritte Aufl.; Tübingen: Mohr, 1926), pp. 213-215.

4. Cf. Some of the older attempts to find a difference between the two phrases in J. S. Candlish, *The Kingdom of God* (Edinburgh: T. and T. Clark, 1884), pp. 371-375.

5. The stages between the original Aramaic teaching and our Greek Gospels are not easy to recover. Some modern scholars have held that our Gospels were originally written in Aramaic before they were translated into their present Greek form. This, however, has not been substantiated. It is likely that the teachings of our Lord were translated in an oral form into Greek before they became incorporated in our present Gospels. Cf. the brief but excellent discussion in F. V. Filson, *Origins of the Gospels* (New York: Abingdon Press, 1938), pp. 56-84. In any case, the Aramaic of Jesus' teaching shows at a number of points. Cf. Mark 7:34, 5:41, 15:34.

most common substitutes was "heaven."[6] The prodigal son phrased his prayer of repentance, "Father, I have sinned against heaven, and in thy sight" (Luke 15:21). Jesus asked the Jews, "The baptism of John, whence was it? from heaven or from men?" (Matt. 21:25). A similar substitution for the name of God is found on the lips of the High Priest when he asked Jesus, "Art thou the Christ, the Son of the Blessed?" (Mark 14:61).

Against this background, the terminology of our Gospels is not difficult to understand. Jesus spoke in Aramaic to the Jewish people. In doing so, he probably employed both expressions at one time or another, but it is likely that he used the "kingdom of heaven" more than the "kingdom of God" because of the Jewish partiality for such a substitution, and he would naturally make his language as appealing to his hearers as possible. Matthew, writing his gospel for Jews, retained this phrase with only a few exceptions, which exceptions suggest that Jesus did not use the one phrase exclusively. Mark and Luke, as well as John, writing to Gentiles, uniformly employed the phraseology which would be more meaningful to their readers than "the kingdom of the heavens," a phrase which would sound to the gentile ear something like "the

---

6. "Heavens" in Hebrew and Aramaic: the singular of the word does not exist. This use of "heaven" is found both in the intertestamental literature and in the talmudic literature. I *Macc.* 3:50, "And they cried aloud toward heaven": 12:15, "for we have the help that is from heaven to help us." *Pirke Aboth* 1:3, "Let the fear of Heaven be upon us"; 2:16, "And let all thy actions be to the name of Heaven." In the Targums, the "kingdom of God" is found in such places as Isa. 31:4, 40:9, 52:7, Micah 4:7, Zech. 14:9. But in the rabbinic literature "kingdom of heaven" is always substituted for the "kingdom of God" (Kuhn in *Theologisches Wörterbuch zum Neuen Testament*, I, 570). The following will illustrate this rabbinic usage: "The name of heaven," "the decrees of heaven," "the mercy of heaven," "the word of heaven," "by the hand of heaven." (G. Dalman, *The Words of Jesus*, p. 219: H. L. Strack and P. Billerbeck, *Kommentar zum Neuen Testament aus Talmud und Midrasch*, I, p. 862). In the latter work, it is pointed out that the word "heaven" never has the definite article as it would in normal Semitic usage because the word has practically become a proper name.

kingdom of the skies" or "the kingdom of the clouds" would sound to us.

This is the simplest explanation and adequately accounts for the data in the Gospels. If any difference is to be sought, one can go no further than does Zahn when he says that the kingdom of heaven indicates "that the new and final order of things in Israel and the world in which God will truly be king does not come from the earth but from heaven, and is established not through human activity but through divine acts. The best commentary to this is provided in the words of Jesus in John 18:36f."[7]

The kingdom which Jesus preached

What was the meaning of Jesus' offer of the kingdom to Israel? Jesus offered to Israel the same kingdom which he now offers to both Jew and Gentile. We must recall the basic significance of *basileia*. Jesus announced that the sovereignty of God was to be manifested in a new activity which was itself the guarantee of its final and perfect consummation. The kingdom of Satan was about to be invaded. Indeed, it was invaded by the very presence of the King on earth, a fact which was affirmed by his messianic activity, especially the exorcism of demons. The kingdom of God, the kingly power of God, manifested itself with violent power[8] as the demand is laid upon men to render a decision for the kingdom with such utter surrender that it may amount to violence.[9] When such decision is made, it can be said that men "enter into the kingdom of God": i.e., they come within the sphere of his sovereign, saving power (Luke 16:16). In the fullest sense of

---

7. Theodor Zahn, *Das Evangelium des Matthäus*, p. 129. Cf. also *Grundriss der neutestamentlichen Theologie* (Leipzig: Deichert, 1928), pp. 6-7. For a similar distinction see Geerhardus Vos, *The Teaching of Jesus Concerning the Kingdom of God and the Church*, pp. 34-37.
8. Cf. Matthew 11:12, "The kingdom of heaven has been coming violently" (R. S. V. mg.). For this rendering cf. N. B. Stonehouse, *The Witness of Matthew and Mark to Christ* (Philadelphia: The Presbyterian Guardian, 1944), pp. 245ff., and the literature there cited.
9. Cf. Luke 9:23-62, 9:57-62, 14:26, Matt. 19:21.

the word, that is, as the realm in which the reign of God is perfectly realized, the kingdom is never said to have come. That coming is always future and will not be experienced until after the Parousia of Christ as the glorious King. But the kingdom in the abstract sense of the word, as the kingly rule and sovereignty of God manifesting itself in a new order of divine government in the spiritual realm, was announced by Jesus as having come near (*eggiken* Matt. 3:2, 4:17, 10:7), as having arrived (*ephthasen*, Matt. 12:28, Luke 11:20).[10]

Jesus offered to men a new experience of God's reign. Eventually this reign is to be externally manifested, first in this world when during the millennium it becomes the realm in which his reign is realized, and finally in the age to come. But that future earthly realm was not what Jesus offered to Israel. Before the kingdom is to be thus realized on the earth or in the age to come, it must come to men as a present spiritual reality, to be realized here and now in the sphere of their own lives. God may now reign within them as it was never before possible. Only those who submit themselves to this new manifestation of God's kingdom, and who render a decision for Christ and the kingdom will enter the future kingdom when it comes. The present spiritual kingdom prepares men for the future glorious kingdom, but it is one and the same kingdom, the rule of the one sovereign God.

---

10. Cf. Theodor Zahn, *Das Evangelium des Matthäus*, pp. 124-125. The word *ephthasen* does not mean "to have arrived" in the fullest sense of the word as the Realized Eschatologists interpret it (cf. C. H. Dodd, *The Parables of the Kingdom*, London: Nisbet, 1936, pp. 43-48, and our discussion above pp. 87-88), thus eliminating the future eschatological aspect of the kingdom. It means "the kingdom of God has just reached you," without the full experience of all that the kingdom is to involve. The kingdom as the reign of God *fully realized* in all human relationships is future; but the kingdom as the reign of God to be realized in personal experience has come to men now in the person and mission of Christ. So the kingdom is yet to come, but its powers have already come. Cf. the excellent linguistic discussion in K. W. Clark, "Realized Eschatology," *J. B. L.*, LIX (1940), pp. 367-383. Professor Clark does not permit *ephthasen* as much significance with reference to the kingdom of God as the illustrations which he cites require. The word *does* mean that in some sense or other, the kingdom *has arrived*.

The kingdom and the Sermon on the Mount

Against this background the Sermon on the Mount is to be interpreted. It delineates the righteousness which is demanded of those who experience God's kingly power. Those in whose lives God now reigns, those who become the citizens of the kingdom of God are to have a new righteousness. This righteousness of the kingdom is to exceed that of the Scribes and Pharisees (Matt. 5:20), not however by imposing upon its adherents an outward legalistic standard which was more inclusive and which demanded a more exact performance than did the scribal law. The essential character of scribal righteousness was that it was designed to cover every experience of life and leave no area outside of the control of the explicit law of God. For every activity in which a man could engage, the law had a dictum as to the will of God. How can any legalism exceed this?

The new kingdom righteousness exceeds the scribal righteousness by reaching to a man's motives, by requiring more than a proper outward conduct, by demanding an inner righteousness as well. It is with this *new principle* of righteousness that the Sermon on the Mount is concerned. This is proved by the applications which Jesus made of the new righteousness. The old law said, Do not kill; the new law says, Do not be angry, for anger is the source of murder. The old law said, Do not commit adultery; the new law says, Do not lust, for lust is the source of adultery. How can legalism control anger and lust? These are matters of the heart and of inner motive; and law, properly speaking, can control only one's actions. But the new righteousness, the reign of God in a man's life, demands precisely an inner righteousness, a righteousness of the heart. The will of God is concerned with what a man is as the source of what he does. The entire Sermon on the Mount must be interpreted by this principle. We *are* to pray, "Forgive us our debts as we forgive our debtors." A tree is known by its fruits, and a good tree must bear good fruits (Matt. 7:16-20). If a man does not know how to forgive his fellow men their trivial offenses against him, how can he make any just claim that he has been forgiven the immeasurable debt of his sin against God? Such a profession is mockery. Jesus himself taught that in another context (Matt. 18:23-35). A readiness to forgive is a proof that one has been forgiven.

While the Sermon on the Mount does not indicate how this righteousness is to be obtained, it makes it very clear that when the reign of God is realized in the realm of personal experience, that reign will result in a new and inner righteousness, the very righteousness of God himself, for it is *God who reigns* within.

The Sermon on the Mount furthermore teaches that only those who accept the present manifestation of the rule of God and so realize within themselves the new righteousness of God shall have entrance into the consummated kingdom of God of the future. It is not enough to have an external righteousness. It is not enough to have rendered service in the name of Christ. Only those who surrender their hearts to the newly manifested reign of God, who thereby come to possess the inner righteousness which the old law could not produce, will have access to the final glorious kingdom when it shall come. Others who have only an external, formal righteousness, who on this ground will claim a place in the kingdom, will be cast out.

The kingdom and the parables

The parables also are to be interpreted against this same background. It is quite true that the Old Testament prophecies look forward primarily to the earthly aspect of the kingdom. Basing their interpretation upon such prophecies, the Jewish people expected a kingdom of an outward, political, earthly sort. As we have already seen, they failed to understand the prophecies that indicated that the Messiah should come in humility to suffer and die before he should come in power and glory to reign. Similarly, they anticipated only the kingdom in its external earthly aspect. They were more justified in this interpretation than in their failure to understand the prophecies of a suffering Messiah, for the prophets do not have much to say about the kingdom except in its earthly manifestation.

In the midst of his ministry Jesus began to teach his disciples that the Old Testament prophetic ideal was not at once to be fulfilled and that the kingdom was not immediately to be manifested in the fullness of its power. This is the "mystery" of the kingdom,[11] a truth which God has not previously made known to men. This truth is that before the final glorious manifestation of the kingdom when its sway would encompass all the earth and all human relationships, when the Messiah-King would reign visibly over the earth, there is to intervene a different manifestation of the kingdom in a spiritual form, within the hearts of men.

The first two parables have to do with the reception of this new message of the kingdom in the world: it is not to be always and everywhere successful. The parable of the soils teaches that the kingdom, the reign of God, is not now to come upon men forcibly but must be accepted by the individual that it may take root in his heart; it must be received as soil receives seed. However, not all hearts will receive it. The kingdom is not to experience a uniform success. The second parable teaches that the kingdom is not at once coming in a catastrophic manifestation of judgment upon those who do not accept it. Such a judgment will occur in the future when the Son of Man shall come. Meanwhile, the sons of the kingdom,

---

11. The phrase coined by the dispensational interpretation, "the kingdom in its mystery form," is not a biblical expression. The parables do not speak of the kingdom in a "mystery form," they speak of the mystery of the kingdom, a truth about the kingdom which has not previously been revealed (Rom. 16:25-26).

those who receive the gospel, and the sons of the evil one are to live together in the world. The final separation is not yet.

It was a new revelation to the disciples that the kingdom of God could come to men and be anything but all-victorious in its coming. The third and fourth parables are designed to assure the disciples that though the kingdom as it is now to be experienced among men is to have only partial success, it must ultimately succeed and be all-encompassing in its sphere. The kingdom at first was to be tiny, insignificant, as the new reign of God was accepted by a handful of men who, by all human standards, counted for nothing; but in the end, the kingdom is to be a great tree, the greatest of all shrubs. Its future form is not to be measured by its initial insignificance. The kingdom is to be like a bit of leaven which when placed in three measures of flour is so imperceptible as to be utterly hid from sight. However, it is ultimately to be manifested, and the *final* result will be a state of things which is everywhere affected by the kingdom of God.

The emphasis of these two parables is not upon the *process,* nor upon the means by which the end is to be accomplished. To take the parable of the leaven out of its context and make it the proof text, as is so often done, for the teaching that the spiritual kingdom is to constitute the entirety of the kingdom which is to grow and extend its influence within the present order of things until the gospel has converted the entire earth and so brought about the golden age is to ignore many other Scriptures which teach that the kingdom will not come apart from the apocalyptic Parousia of Christ. These two parables envisage the totality of the kingdom. The great tree, the complete leavening of the meal, must not be limited to the present age, even though the primary message has to do with this age and the manifestation of the kingdom in it. In the parable of the weeds, the future of the kingdom explicitly looks beyond the Parousia to the time when the righteous will shine in the kingdom of their Father. So we are to understand the parables of the leaven and mustard seed. All seven parables have to do with the kingdom as such, but with special emphasis upon the period preceding its larger manifestation at the Parousia.

The one point which falls under emphasis is that the kingdom of God is now with the coming of Messiah to have an almost insignificant beginning, yet it is not at all insignificant. Such a manifestation of the kingdom was contrary to all Jewish expectations and apparently not in line with the Old Testament teaching. It is nevertheless in very fact the kingdom of God, and as such is certain in the future to be all-encompassing in its scope. The tiny seed will certainly become a great tree. All of the meal will surely become leavened. When and how this is to be accomplished is not the truth which these parables are designed to teach.

The parables of the treasure and of the pearl teach that this kingdom, though in a new and insignificant manifestation, is yet the most valuable treasure in the world and is to be sought at all costs.

The seventh parable teaches that the final separation between the good and bad, the sons of the kingdom and the sons of evil, will not take place until the close of the age, but that it will surely take place even though it seems to be delayed.

Summary

It is time to summarize our findings. We are under no obligation to distinguish between the phrases the kingdom of God and the kingdom of heaven, to find in the former the over-all, universal rule of God and in the latter the rule of God as it concerns the earth. The data in the Gospels indicate that the two terms are interchangeable, and the difference between them is one of linguistic idiom and not of meaning.

Furthermore, we are not to suppose that Jesus offered to the Jews the earthly Davidic kingdom which was postponed because they rejected it and that in its place came the "mystery form" of the kingdom of heaven. Some interpretation of this sort may be necessary if one conceives of the kingdom *only* as the future realm in which the will of God is perfectly done. When the kingdom is interpreted in its true philological sense, as the reign of God, manifested among men in the person of the Savior-King, demanding of men a decision by which they enter into that spiritual realm when God's reign is realized and thus are prepared to enter the future eschatological manifestation of the kingdom, we are delivered from the exegetical and theological difficulties which adhere to the "postponed kingdom" theory. *Nothing was postponed.* It was not God's purpose that the fullness of the kingdom should then come, nor did Jesus offer such a kingdom to men. It is preserved for the consummation. But in the meantime, God is preparing a people who submit themselves here and now to his sovereign reign and so find a new righteousness, an inner righteousness of the heart, the very righteousness of God. Such persons experience the reign of God, the kingdom of God, here and now. To them the kingdom is a present, spiritual reality. The powers of the future kingdom have been realized in present experience. This reign of God, inaugurated by Christ, calls into being a new people. The Jewish people rejected this kingdom, and it was therefore taken from them, who by history, background, and religion ought to have been the "sons of the kingdom" (Matt. 8:12), and was given to a people who would receive it and manifest the righteousness which the kingdom must require (Matt. 21:43). This is the Church, the body of those who have accepted the Christ and so submitted themselves to the reign of God.

As the messiahship of Christ involved two phases, a coming in humility to suffer and die, and a coming in power and glory to reign, so the kingdom is to be manifested in two realms: the present realm of righteousness or salvation when men may accept or reject the kingdom, and the future realm when the powers of the kingdom shall be manifested in visible glory. The former was inaugurated in insignificant beginnings without outward display, and those who accept it are to live intermingled with those who reject it until the consummation. Then the kingdom will be disclosed in a mighty manifestation of power and glory. God's kingdom will come; and the ultimate state will witness the perfect realization of the will of God everywhere and forever.

CHAPTER SEVEN

HOW IS THE KINGDOM IN REVELATION
TWENTY TO BE INTERPRETED?

Outline

Method of procedure
The exegetical approach
Principles of hermeneutics
The exegesis of Revelation 20:1-6

CHAPTER VII

How Is the Kingdom in Revelation Twenty to Be Interpreted?

IN THE preceding chapters we have taken the liberty of anticipating the particular question which we are to discuss now, the question of the millennium and the interpretation of Revelation 20.

Method of procedure

There are two ways of approaching the question of the millennium: the question of its implications and its place in one's system of theology; and the question of what the Scriptures actually teach. It is in the last analysis, of course, impossible to separate these two approaches for the one necessarily involves the other. The former is the theological approach, the latter is the exegetical. There is, however, a necessary order in the way in which the question is to be studied. The exegetical approach must always precede the theological. If there is such a thing as a scientific method in theology, it must pursue this order. One cannot come to the Scriptures with a system of eschatology and fit the records into one's system. One must always ask, What do the Scriptures teach? and then on the basis of the answer derived build his theological system.

The exegetical approach

Our concern at the moment is exegetical. Many theological problems will be raised by the subject of the millennium which we shall not endeavor to answer. To some students several of these problems may seem practically insuperable. Professor Allis concludes his study of dispensationalism and pre-millennialism with such a difficulty. His basic criticism of chiliasm is theological: it raises a problem for which he has found no answer.[1] It is to be granted that systematic theology must be characterized by coherence. However, it is possible to press the desire for apparent coherence to the point where the Scriptures are not exegeted according to a proper hermeneutic. There may be some questions for which we shall never find an adequate answer, especially in the realm of prophecy and eschatology. One suspects that many non-millenarians interpret some passages of the Scriptures as they do, not because they are convinced that inductive exegesis leads to the conclusions they espouse, but because their system does not leave room for any millennial period. They are therefore under the necessity of finding an interpretation for millenarian passages by which their theological system is not impaired. This is improper procedure. Exegesis must always precede theology.

Principles of hermeneutics

Exegesis involves hermeneutics. Most premillenarians have insisted on a "literalistic" interpretation. The Scriptures are not to be spiritualized but are to be interpreted to mean what they say. "Israel" always means the Jewish people and is not to be interpreted to mean the Church. The Old Testament prophecies must be understood literally and cannot be interpreted spiritually to refer to the present dispensation of the spiritual reign of Christ in the lives of Christians. Prophecies which have to do with the Jewish nation and with the land of Palestine must be understood literally. Many students are premillenarians not so much because they feel that a millen-

---

1. Oswald T. Allis, *Prophecy and the Church* (Philadelphia: The Presbyterian and Reformed Pub. Co., 1945), pp. 261-2. See D. H. Kromminga, *The Millennium* (Grand Rapids: Eerdmans, 1948) for an answer to his problem.

nium holds any large place in the New Testament, but because they feel that the Old Testament prophecies demand it.

Amillennialists, on the other hand, accuse premillennialists of employing an inadequate hermeneutic. Professor Rutgers devotes considerable space to castigating premillennialism with the phrase, "exegetical nivelism,"[2] i.e., the reduction of biblical teaching to a single plane of literalism. Professor Berkhof registers his first and strongest objection to the premillennial position because of its allegedly inadequate hermeneutic.[3]

How is an adequate hermeneutic to be deduced? This question is fundamental to our study of eschatology. Can it be maintained that the Scriptures are *always* to be interpreted literally? This seems hardly possible. The Revelation, describing the second advent of Christ, pictures him riding upon a white horse, crowned with many diadems, garbed in a robe dipped in blood, accompanied by the armies of heaven on white horses, coming to smite the nations with a sword which proceeds out of his mouth. No argument is needed to prove that this is symbolic language. Again, the author of Hebrews applies the prophecy of Jeremiah about the new covenant which is to be written upon the hearts of God's people to the covenant which Christ has inaugurated.[4] To insist that this is the covenant to be made in the millennial kingdom with the Jewish nation and thereby to deny that it is the new covenant which has been procured for us by Christ through his death is to violate the entire context of the epistle to the Hebrews. Few would dare to go so far. This passage alone proves that the Old Testament prophecies do indeed have a spiritual fulfillment in the Church, for the prophecy quoted in Hebrews is, in Jeremiah 31, addressed to the house of Israel and Judah.

----

2. William H. Rutgers, *Premillennialism in America* (Goes, Holland: Oosterbaan and Le Cointre, 1930), pp. 136-150.
3. L. Berkhof, *The Kingdom of God* (Grand Rapids: Eerdmans, 1951), pp. 160-166.
4. Hebrews 8:6-13.

The present writer is ready to agree with the amillennialists that there is only one place to find a hermeneutic: in the New Testament. Berkhof is entirely correct in saying that "the main guide to the interpretation of the Old Testament is certainly to be found in the New."[5]

R. B. Jones has written a book largely devoted to the application of this principle.[6] Certainly, if the same Holy Spirit inspired both the New Testament and the Old Testament, we are safe in seeking to discover how the inspiring Spirit interprets the inspired Scripture and in employing the principles so deduced in the interpretation of prophecies as yet unfulfilled. Dr. Jones uses I Corinthians 15:42-57 as the basis for his study and of this passage, verse 46 is the heart: "That is not first which is spiritual, but that which is natural; then that which is spiritual." In this he finds the story of the written revelation,[7] and therefore concludes that "the so-called 'spiritual' principle of interpretation, rather than the literal principle, is correct and has the witness of apostolic practice."[8] This language makes Dr. Jones liable to a serious misunderstanding. It is quite true that the work of Christ brings to men a new world of spiritual realities. Our discussion of the kingdom of God as a present spiritual reality affirms that fact.[9] Furthermore, we are ready to agree that the future kingdom of God is to be a "spiritual" kingdom in the sense that it will involve the application of the spiritual powers of God's sovereign rule to the world of men and affairs. But to assert, as Dr. Jones seems to do, that we are to interpret all of eschatology "spiritually" rather than literally is logically to reduce the second coming of Christ to a spiritual and not to a literal coming, to interpret the resurrection as a "spiritual" resurrection and not

5. L. Berkhof, *The Kingdom of God*, p. 160.

6. Russell Bradley Jones, *The Things Which Shall Be Hereafter* (Nashville: Broadman Press, 1947).

7. *Ibid.*, p. 55.

8. *Ibid.*, p. 64.

9. Cf. *supra* pp. 85-94.

a literal one,[10] and to void eschatology of literal reality. Those who would insist upon such a consistent and thorough-going "spiritual" interpretation of eschatology must make their peace with the position in which the entire content of apocalyptic prophecy is spiritualized.[11]

Our point of departure must be the way the New Testament interprets the Old Testament. When we study the prophecies with reference to the first advent of Christ we are at once impressed that while some of them are interpreted spiritually,[12] the majority of these prophecies that were fulfilled in the birth, life, and death of Christ were fulfilled with amazing literalness. Although the intellectual atmosphere of our times is against it, this literal fulfillment of biblical prophecy remains to an open mind a strong apologetic for the supernatural character of the Scriptures. If then we take this as our basic hermeneutic, we shall conclude that some prophecies which have to do with the complex of events surrounding the second advent of Christ will be fulfilled only in a spiritual sense, but

---

10. The "spiritual body" of I Corinthians 15:44 is not a body made of spirit, any more than the "natural" (literally, *psychical*) body is a body made of *psyche*. Dr. Jones recognizes this. However, it is a *literal, real body*, even though it is adapted to the new order of existence which shall be inaugurated at the resurrection for those who experience it.

11. Cf. C. J. Wright, *The Eternal Kingdom* (London: James Clarke, n. d.), chapter V. "We ourselves, in our myopic endeavours to read into the teaching of our Lord materialistic notions of 'the end,' find spurious dilemmas in that teaching. We forget that poetry is not prose, and that art is not logic" (p. 117). "Yet this use of symbol, metaphor, parable and allegory does not obviate misunderstanding. . . . We must seek to penetrate behind the letter of His speech to the living spirit, behind the form to the mind that informs, behind the sign to the thing signified. . . . (The Divine Rule) comes by inward renewal, not by external coercive act" (pp. 119-120). "When humanity has come to the stature of the 'perfect man in Christ Jesus' then will the Kingdom have fully come" (p. 122). "How can we babble about 'times and seasons' in the presence of Truth? The Kingdom of God *is*: Its victory is sure: but how or when no man knows" (pp. 126-127).

12. John the Baptist was Elijah who was to precede the coming of Christ (Matt. 11:14), but surely not Elijah reincarnate: he was Elijah in a spiritual sense. John certainly did not engage in any road-building operations in fulfillment of Isaiah 40:3ff. (Luke 3:4-6). Jesus is the Lamb of God (John 3:36) in a spiritual sense. Cf. Russell Bradley Jones, *The Things Which Shall Be Hereafter*, pp. 41-50 for other illustrations.

that others will be fulfilled literally. There is no uniform principle of spiritual, symbolical interpretation to be deduced from the New Testament treatment of the Old Testament. Some prophecies may have a present spiritual interpretation, and also a future literal interpretation which will be simply a broader application of the spiritual significance involved.

It is difficult to feel any force in Dr. Berkhof's position at this point.

> We are told that all prophecies fulfilled in the past, received a literal fulfillment; and that, therefore, the presumption is that all prophecies will be so fulfilled. However, though it was but natural that prophecies referring to the *near* future should be fulfilled in the exact form in which they were uttered, this is not to be expected *a priori,* nor is it likely in the case of prophecies pertaining to the *distant* future, to a new dispensation with greatly altered conditions.[13]

To this, three things are to be said. First, we may not assume at the outset, as Dr. Berkhof seems to do, that which we seek to discover: viz., the degree to which the future dispensation will be one of greatly altered conditions. Secondly, from the perspective of the Old Testament prophets, it is difficult to see the validity of the distinction between the near future and the distant future as applying to the first and the second coming of Christ. Let us suppose that the difference is that between 500 years and 2500 years. In either case, the future events are in the distant future so far as the prophets are concerned. This fact is sustained by the well known "prophetic perspective" by which the two advents of Christ are foreseen as a single, great event. Finally, the conclusion which is deduced by such an examination of the New Testament treatment of the Old Testament is not *a priori* reasoning. It is precisely the opposite to that; it is a conclusion based on inductive study.

---

13. L. Berkhof, *op. cit.,* p. 165 (italics ours).

We must conclude therefore that there is no *single* interpretation in the study of prophecy, either literal or spiritual. The same laws of hermeneutics and exegesis are to be employed which are used elsewhere. Unless there is some reason intrinsic within the text itself which requires a symbolical interpretation, or unless there are other Scriptures which interpret a parallel prophecy in a symbolic sense, we are required to employ a natural, literal interpretation. The future kingdom will indeed be "spiritual" in that it will be the application of the supernatural power of God to the world and to human society, but such a spiritual interpretation does not empty future events of their literal reality.

The exegesis of Revelation 20:1-6

We must now turn to a consideration of the interpretation of Revelation 20:1-6. It will be impossible to study each word exhaustively, but that will not be necessary for our present purpose. There is really only one question which must be answered. Verses four and five read, "They (the persons mentioned earlier in verse 4) lived, and reigned with Christ a thousand years. The rest of the dead lived not until the thousand years should be finished. This is the first resurrection." What does it mean to "live"? The entire interpretation of the passage hangs upon the one question of whether the first "living" and the "living" of the rest of the dead means the same thing, viz., bodily resurrection. What is the first resurrection? Is it literal, a resurrection of the body, or "spiritual," a resurrection of the soul? If we can find the answer to this question, we shall have the key to the solution of the millennial question in this passage.

We may approach the matter by stating briefly the two interpretations. The first is the natural interpretation of the words. There are two resurrections of the dead, one preceding and one following the thousand year reign of Christ. Those who are raised before the thousand years share Christ's reign over the earth, during which period Satan is bound and incarcerated in a bottomless pit. The rest of the dead are not raised until the termination of this millennial reign of Christ and his saints. In this interpretation, the thousand years is a period of time which begins with the second advent of Christ and the first stage of the resurrection of the dead. It is entirely future, and is seen as a period of time intervening between the consummation of this age and the inauguration of the final, eternal age to come.

The other interpretation is the so-called "spiritual" one, although the term is not altogether satisfactory. The literal is really not less spiritual than any other; non-literal would perhaps be a better expression. This interpretation is found in two forms, both of which understand the first resurrection in a spiritual sense. One goes back to Augustine and identifies the millennium with the entire course of the present church age. The other understands the thousand years in a purely symbolical fashion indicating perfection and completeness, having no reference to time.

This latter view has not won wide acceptance and seems to be comparatively recent. This view holds that the thousand years is not a symbol of a period of time but of an idea: the idea of the completeness of the victory of God's kingdom over Anti-christ, the world-powers, and the Devil. The victory of the Lord is absolutely comprehensive. The lordship of Christ and of his saints, so long as it lasts, is ecumenical; the binding of Satan, so long as it continues, renders him impotent for the entire sphere of the *oikoumene,* for the entire extent of historical existence. No temporal implication of any sort is intended.[14]

---

14. Cf. Th. Klieforth, *Die Offenbarung Johannes* (Leipzig: Dörffling und Franke, 1874), III, pp. 284-286. Approximately the same view will be found in Fr. Düsterdieck, *A Critical and Exegetical Handbook to the Revelation of John* (H. A. W. Meyer, ed.; E. T.; New York: Funk and Wagnalls, 1887), p. 470; William Milligan, *The Book of Revelation* in *The Expositor's Bible* (Reprinted by Eerdmans, 1947), VI, pp. 913-915. It should be noted that not all millennialists insist upon an absolutely literal interpretation of the thousand years. It may represent a temporal inter-regnum of Christ and yet not involve a thousand calendar years. Cf. J. P. Lange, *The Revelation of John* (E. T., New York: Scribner's, 1874), pp. 349-352.

What we may call the Augustinian view identifies the thousand years with the period between the two advents of Christ. Augustine understood the living and reigning with Christ of the spiritual resurrection of dead souls and quoted Colossians 3:1 to illustrate this resurrection. The thrones refer to the rulers' places in the Church and the persons are those by whom it is governed. The souls represent the believing martyrs who, according to Augustine, together with the living saints constitute the Church of Christ.[15] This view may sometimes be found in modern writers.[16]

Most interpreters who spiritualize the thousand years follow a modification of Augustine's view and place the emphasis not upon the spiritual life of believers on earth but upon the blessedness of the intermediate state to be experienced by those who possess eternal life who are called upon (or who are ready to be called upon) to lay down their lives for Christ. Such martyrs and confessors, contrary to external appearances, do not really die; rather, they enter into the fullness of life and blessing as they reign with Christ in the intermediate state. The vision is one of the perfect blessedness of the souls of the saved in Paradise between the two advents of Christ.[17]

The crux of the entire exegetical problem is the meaning of the one word: *ezesan*. At the beginning of the thousand

---

15. *City of God*, XX, 6-9.

16. Cf. Floyd E. Hamilton, *The Basis of Millennial Faith* (Grand Rapids: Eerdmans, 1942), pp. 128-134.

17. Cf. Henry Barclay Swete, *The Apocalypse of St. John* (London: Macmillan, 1917), pp. 261-267; R. C. H. Lenski, *The Interpretation of St. John's Revelation* (Columbus, Ohio: Wartburg Press, 1943), pp. 578-590; B. B. Warfield, *Biblical Doctrines* (New York: Oxford, 1929), pp. 648-664; James H. Snowden, *The Coming of the Lord: Will it be Premillennial?* (New York: Macmillan, 1919), pp. 181-184; W. Hendriksen, *More Than Conquerors* (Grand Rapids: Baker's, 1940), pp. 230-232; William Masselink, *Why Thousand Years?* (Grand Rapids: Eerdmans, 1930), pp. 200-208; Russell Bradley Jones, *The Things Which Shall Be Hereafter* (Nashville: Broadman, 1947), pp. 145-156; George L. Murray, *Millennial Studies* (Grand Rapids: Baker, 1948), pp. 175-185.

years, some people *ezesan* and reign with Christ. At the end of the thousand years, the rest of the dead *ezesan*. Most exegetes will agree that the second *ezesan* refers to the literal resurrection of the "rest of the dead" and might be translated, "they came to life again" as does the Revised Standard Version. The question is, can the former· *ezesan* mean something different? Can it refer to a spiritual resurrection when the second word refers to a literal resurrection?

No objection can be raised on the ground that it is not possible to speak of a spiritual and of a literal reality in the same context. Jesus does this very thing in speaking of the dead and of the resurrection.

> Verily, verily, I say unto you, The hour cometh, and now is, when the dead shall hear the voice of the Son of God; and they that hear shall live. For as the Father hath life in himself, even so gave he to the Son also to have life in himself; and he gave him authority to execute judgment, because he is a son of man. Marvel not at this; for the hour cometh, in which all that are in the tombs shall hear his voice, and shall come forth; they that have done good, unto the resurrection of life; and they that have done evil, unto the resurrection of judgment.[18]

However, this passage does not provide a true analogy to the passage in the Apocalypse. There is this all-important difference: in the Gospel, the context itself provides the clues for the spiritual interpretation in the one instance and the literal in the other. Concerning the first group who are to live, *the hour has already come*. This saying makes it clear that the reference is to those who are spiritually dead and who enter into life upon hearing the voice of the Son of God. The second group, however, are in the tombs, i.e., they are not the spiritually dead but the physically dead. Such dead are to be brought

---

18. John 5:25-29.

back to life again. Part of them will experience a resurrection of life, i.e., a bodily resurrection which will lead them to the full expression of the spiritual life which is already theirs. The rest will be revived to a resurrection of condemnation, i.e., to the execution of the decree of divine judgment which rests upon them already because they have rejected the Son of God and the life he came to bring (John 3:18, 36). The language of these words makes it indubitable that Jesus wishes his hearers to know that he is speaking of two experiences of "living"; a present spiritual resurrection, and a future bodily resurrection.

A similar transfer from the spiritual to the literal is found in Luke 9:60, "leave the dead to bury their own dead." This however provides no analogy for the interpretation of Revelation 20:4-5, for again, the clue to the correct interpretation of Luke 9:60 is found in the very passage itself. *The statement is meaningless* without such a variation in interpretation; it is therefore obviously intended. No such problem exists in Revelation 20; the language makes perfectly good sense without taking either word spiritually, and we are not therefore required to do so as we are in Luke 9:60.

Another illustration is found in Luke 9:24. "For whosoever would save his life shall lose it; but whosoever shall lose his life for my sake, the same shall save it." In neither case is the word for life, *zoe* used, but the word for soul, *psyche*. This word in biblical Greek is regularly used with a lower and a higher reference in different contexts, sometimes indicating the physical life and sometimes the real self.[19] The character of this verse *demands* that the dual reference be here recognized. No such demand is laid upon the reader by Revelation 20:4-6. If such a dual reference is not read into the passage, it would never be recognized in the passage itself.

The same principle is true of John 11:25-6, where dying and living are clearly physical and spiritual; but the variation is

19. Cf. H. B. Swete, *The Gospel According to St. Mark* (London: Macmillan, 1909, reprinted, Eerdmans, 1951), pp. 182-3.

discovered within the passage itself and not by interpreting it in the light of other passages.

In these several passages there is a clue which is required by the context or by the words themselves which suggests and requires the literal interpretation on the one hand, and the spiritual on the other. But in Revelation 20:4-6, *there is no such contextual clue for a similar variation of interpretation.* The language of the passage is quite clear and unambiguous. There is no necessity to interpret either word spiritually in order to introduce meaning to the passage. At the beginning of the millennial period, part of the dead come to life; at its conclusion, the rest of the dead come to life. There is no evident play upon words here. The passage makes perfectly good sense when interpreted literally. We must conclude therefore that the passages cited above are not truly analogous, and do not provide sufficient justification for interpreting the first *ezesan* spiritually and the second literally. Natural, inductive exegesis suggests that both words are to be taken in the same way, referring to a literal resurrection. We can do no better than to repeat the oft-quoted words of Henry Alford,

> If, in a passage where *two resurrections* are mentioned, where certain *psychai ezesan* at the first, and the rest of the *nekroi ezesan* only at the end of a specified period after that first, — if in such a passage the first resurrection may be understood to mean *spiritual* rising with Christ, while the second means *literal* rising from the grave; — then there is an end of all significance in language, and Scripture is wiped out as a definite testimony to anything.[20]

Since it is not required by the context itself, the only legitimate reason for employing first a spiritual and then a literal

---

20. Henry Alford, *The Greek Testament* (Boston: Lee and Shepard, 1872), IV. p. 732.

hermeneutic in this passage would be that the teachings of the rest of the Scripture demand it. This is the reason usually given, and it will be discussed below.[21] We are concerned at the moment only to show that this procedure is neither required, nor suggested by the passage itself.

It is sometimes claimed that we are here dealing with apocalyptic literature and that a different hermeneutic is therefore demanded. Professor Swete, in his excellent commentary, says that to interpret the first *ezesan* of a bodily resurrection "is to interpret apocalyptic prophecy by methods of exegesis which are proper to ordinary narrative."[22] This is a revealing statement, for it admits that the spiritual interpretation departs from the proper principles of hermeneutics because this is literature of a different type to which the ordinary rules of hermeneutics cannot apply. Granted that the Revelation belongs to the genus of apocalyptic literature and is the only instance of its kind in the New Testament, this is not to affirm that the ordinary laws of hermeneutics must be abandoned. It means only that symbol must be recognized wherever symbols are obviously intended.[23]

It is, of course, obvious that much of the Revelation is portrayed in symbolic concepts. As a matter of fact, no one interprets the Revelation *throughout in a literal manner.* Many millenarians will not insist that the earthly reign of Christ is to be of exactly 1000 years duration. The 1000 years may well be a symbol for a long period of time, the exact

---

21. Cf. pp. 169ff.
22. H. B. Swete, *The Apocalypse of St. John* (London: Macmillan, 1909; reprinted, Eerdmans, 1951), p. 263.
23. "The fundamental fault of the interpretations which follow even remotely this theory is that they mistake the nature of apocalyptic prophecy, and read into the vision of our Apocalyptist here a meaning of which he gives no intimation and which is at variance with his language. *Apocalyptic prophecy is not allegory* (italics ours), and in our passage it is not possible upon any sound principles of exegesis to take the first resurrection as different *in kind* from that of 'the rest,' v. 5, which is described in vv. 12-13." I. T. Beckwith, *The Apocalypse of John* (New York: Macmillan, 1919), p. 738.

extent of which is unknown. No one believes that four different colored horsemen ever have or ever shall ride across the earth; these are obviously symbols. Yet even the symbols are representative of historical objective events, movements, and persons, and are not confined to spiritual experience, i.e., to experiences within the soul of man. Whether the Beast of Revelation 13 refers to a future personal Anti-Christ, or to the Papacy, it refers to some historic personage or institution and not to a merely spiritual reality. The doom of Babylon depicted in chapter 19 refers to the actual judgment and overthrow of a godless civilization, and not to some spiritual reality. The coming of the "King of kings and Lord of lords" in Revelation 19 depicts the actual, literal, personal return of Christ in victory to the earth. Even those who like Jones and Berkhof, insist upon consistent "spiritual" interpretation will not go so far as to spiritualize the second coming of Christ.

The recognition of the symbolic language of the Apocalypse does not carry with it the corollary that *every phrase* must involve a symbol. Swete seems to require this when he says, "The symbolism of the Book is opposed to a literal understanding of the Thousand Years and of the resurrection and the reign of the Saints with Christ."[24]

To insist upon this *requires the insistence that "the rest of the dead ezesan" also involves a symbol.* Upon this we must insist, for there is no internal evidence that any variation in the meaning of the words is intended. The same thing happens to part of the dead which later happens to the rest of the dead. If the first resurrection is a spiritual resurrection, then the second resurrection must also refer to a spiritual and not to a bodily resurrection, and few will insist on that.[26] If on

---

24. *Op. cit.*, p. 266.

26. This is precisely what Albertus Pieters does, for he feels the force of Alford's criticism but cannot accept the chiliastic view. Cf. *The Lamb, The Woman and the Dragon* (Grand Rapids: Zondervan, 1937, reissued as *Studies in the Revelation of St. John*, Eerdmans, 1950), pp. 318-323.

the other hand, the rest of the dead experience a literal resurrection at the end of the thousand years, then by all the laws of hermeneutics and interpretation, the first resurrection which part of the dead experience at the beginning of the thousand years must also be a literal, bodily resurrection.[27]

Thus by inductive exegesis, beginning with the New Testament and not with the Old, we find that we are required to include in our outline of future events two resurrections of the dead separated by an extended period of time during which Christ and those who experience the first resurrection reign together.

This interpretation is supported by the use of the same word *ezesan* in 2:8 and 13:14 where it refers to men who died and who "came to life again." Again, the twenty-four elders sang of the redeemed, "thou . . . hast made them a kingdom and priests to our God, and they shall reign on earth."[28]

The history of interpretation would suggest that any interpretation of Revelation 20 other than the natural one arises not from inductive exegetical studies, but from theological presuppositions of an anti-millenarian character. The first anti-millenarians disparaged the natural interpretation of Revelation, not for exegetical reasons because they thought the book did not teach a millennium, but for theological reasons because they did not like millennial doctrine.[29] K. L. Schmidt says

---

27. "If the true sense be *not* the literal one, it is safest to regard it as being as yet undiscovered." W. H. Simcox, *The Revelation of St. John the Divine* (Cambridge: University Press, 1909), p. 237.

28. Rev. 5:10, Revised Standard Version. The textual problem as to whether we should read "they shall reign" or "they reign" does not greatly affect the significance of the passage. The point is that the saints reign on earth, not in heaven. If the reading is present, the verse is a proleptic reference to the future millennial reign. Cf. R. H. Charles, *A Critical and Exegetical Commentary on the Revelation of St. John* (New York: Scribner's, 1920), I, p. 148.

29. Cf. above pp. 23-25, 156-158.

that the man[30] who refuses to find an intermediary stage between the two ages in Revelation 20 approaches the text with preconceived ideas, and gains from it neither the exact sense nor the value.[31]   So it would seem.

---

30. Schmidt is referring in particular to Paul Althaus' position in *Die letzten Dinge* (Gütersloh: Bertelsmann, 1933, 4 Aufl.), pp. 286-306. (Cf. 5 Aufl.; 1949, pp. 297-318.)

31. K. L. Schmidt, *Le Probleme du Christianisme primitif* (Paris: Leroux, 1938), pp. 84-85.

CHAPTER EIGHT

OBJECTIONS TO THE MILLENNIAL INTERPRETATION

Outline

THE "JEWISHNESS" OF THE MILLENNIAL INTERPRETATION

The millennial interpretation in the Early Fathers

Chiliasm in Jewish apocalyptic

Christian and Jewish chiliasm

Parallels between Jewish and Christian eschatology

THE SILENCE OF THE OTHER NEW TESTAMENT BOOKS

The weakness of this objection

The evidence of the Gospels

The evidence of the Epistles

Progressive Revelation

CONCLUSION

CHAPTER VIII

Objections to the Millennial Interpretation

HAVING established that an inductive study of Revelation 20 leads to a hermeneutic which interprets the millennium as a literal reign of Christ between the two resurrections, we must now give consideration to several of the most important objections which have been raised against this interpretation.

THE "JEWISHNESS" OF THE MILLENNIAL INTERPRETATION

The first and most important objection is addressed to the character of the literal interpretation itself. Non-millenarians often charge the literal interpretation with being "Jewish" and therefore non-Scriptural. This objection was not created by modern amillenarians,[1] but is practically as old as the Christian Church. Caius of Rome (*cir.* 200) did not like the chiliasm which was taught by the Montanist sect. He therefore attributed the millennial doctrine to the Jewish Gnostic Cerinthus rather than to the Scriptures, in order apparently to undermine its biblical authority.[2] Origen labeled the literal exegesis as Jewish,[3] as have many subsequent adherents of the spiritual interpretation. In two creedal statements of the

1. Cf. Oswald T. Allis, *Prophecy and the Church* (Philadelphia: The Presbyterian and Reformed Pub. Co., 1945), p. 287; William H. Rutgers, *Premillennialism in America* (Goes, Holland: Oosterbaan and Le Cointre, 1930), pp. 132-136; James H. Snowden, *The Coming of the Lord: Will It Be Premillennial?* (New York: Macmillan, 1919), pp. 192-219; Russell Bradley Jones, *The Things Which Shall Be Hereafter* (Nashville: Broadman Press, 1947), pp. 156-161.
2. Eusebius, *H. E.,* III, xxviii, 2.
3. *De Principiis* II, xi, 2-3.

Reformation, chiliasm was excluded from the body of acceptable doctrine. The Augsburg Confession of 1530 castigated this interpretation by the phrase *Judaices opiniones* (XVII), and the Second Helvetic Confession of 1566 called millennial hopes *Judaica somnia* (XI, 14). Many modern adherents of the Reformed faith have followed the lead of these Confessions.

The implication of this position is that the literal interpretation of the millennium is neither the natural nor the correct one. The true interpretation is the spiritual view which sees it as the spiritual reign of Christ and his saints. We are led to suppose that this view would have been normative in the Church if it had not been for the influence of Jewish apocalypses. John the Apostle supposedly did not mean to teach that Christ was to reign literally on the earth, and those to whom the Apocalypse was written did not understand him so to teach. However, there were abroad Jewish apocalypses which taught that there was one day to be an earthly kingdom. Christians were influenced by these non-Christian books to misunderstand the Apocalypse by interpreting it in light of the views which were found in the non-canonical apocalypses. Thus the true meaning of the millennium was lost sight of and in its place was substituted a Jewish doctrine of an earthly kingdom which is really a perversion of the truth.

According to this view, the spiritual interpretation goes back to the Revelation, while the literal interpretation does not stem from the Revelation but was created by Christians in the first century who were under the influence of Jewish apocalyptic. The true interpretation was lost sight of for several centuries and was not recovered until the times of Augustine.

The millennial interpretation in the Early Fathers

It is very strange, however, if the spiritual interpretation is the true and therefore the original one, that these Jewish apocalypses had such an extensive influence that they so completely crowded out the true interpretation as to obliterate it completely. Certainly we would expect to find some traces of this true interpretation of the millennium somewhere in the first two centuries. Nothing of the sort is to be found, and the spiritual interpretation, when it finally appears in Augustine, seems to be not the recovery of a lost truth, but *the creation of an interpretation which had not previously existed.*

On the other hand millennial doctrine seems to have been widely prevalent.[4] This cannot be appreciated merely by endeavoring to count the adherents of the position on the one hand and those who do not espouse it on the other. As a matter of fact, no judgment in this area of the history of doctrine can be final, for our sources are so fragmentary that we cannot really recreate the history of thought during the first years of church history. Many such questions cannot be settled with certainty; one can only draw inferences from a critical study of the fragmentary literature.

It is to be admitted that only a few of the early Fathers say anything specifically about an earthly millennial reign of Christ. This however is not necessarily to be construed as

---

4. The extent to which chiliasm was entertained in the early centuries of the Church has been widely discussed, both by critical and uncritical scholars. Premillenarians have claimed practically every Church Father for their position, and amillenarians have stressed the fact that only a few of the Fathers expressly affirm the doctrine. Cf. D. T. Taylor, *The Voice of the Church on the Coming and Kingdom of the Redeemer* (Third edition; Philadelphia, 1856), chapters 3 and 4; (a later edition was published under the name *The Reign of Christ on Earth*, London, 1882); C. A. Briggs, "The Origin and History of Premillenarianism," *Lutheran Quarterly* IX (1879), pp. 207-245; Albertus Pieters, "Chiliasm in the Writings of the Apostolic Fathers," *The Calvin Forum*, IV (1938), pp. 9-11, 37-39; I. M. Haldeman, *The History of the Doctrine of Our Lord's Return* (a pamphlet lacking publication data); L. S. Chafer, *Systematic Theology* (Dallas: Dallas Seminary Press, 1948), IV, pp. 267-277; M. V. Ermoni, "Les phases successives de l'erreur millenariste," *Revue des Questions Historique LXX* (1901), pp. 353-388 (Catholic); D. H. Kromminga, *The Millennium in the Church* (Grand Rapids: Eerdmans, 1945), pp. 41-124; N. B. Stonehouse, *The Apocalypse in the Ancient Church* (Goes, Holland: Oosterbaan and Le Cointre, 1929), pp. 13-25; A. Harnack, "Millennium," *Encyclopaedia Britannica*, 9th ed.; XVI, pp. 328-330; Léon Gry, *Le millénarisme dans ses origines et son développement* (Paris: Picard, 1904).

evidence against their belief in the doctrine. Most of the Fathers do not mention it one way or the other and cannot be shown to be either premillenarians or amillenarians. They have very little to say about eschatology in any form. Whenever the kingdom of God is mentioned, it is a future apocalyptic kingdom. We read in the homily known as *II Clement,* "Let us then wait for the kingdom of God, from hour to hour, in love and righteousness, seeing that we know not the day of the appearing of God."[5] At the Lord's Supper, the author of the *Didache* suggests the following prayer: "Remember, Lord, thy Church, to deliver it from all evil and to make it perfect in thy love, and gather it together in its holiness from the four winds to thy kingdom which thou has prepared for it. . . . Maranatha, Amen."[6] In both of these references, the kingdom is a future blessing to be realized at the coming of Christ and could refer either to a millennium or to the final salvation. Its specific character is not defined.

It is also to be admitted that we sometimes find hostility to the doctrine of an earthly kingdom; but such hostility is directed mainly against the extreme form of chiliasm taught by the Montanists or by men like Papias. The amillennialism which we find before Augustine is negative. It consists of opposition to contemporary chiliastic teachings and does not suggest an alternative interpretation, as Augustine did. Justin Martyr (*cir.* 150) knew of "many who belong to the pure and pious faith, and are true Christians, (who) think otherwise,"[7] but he does not indicate the grounds on which the millennial doctrine was rejected. Around 170 A.D. there arose a sect in Asia Minor who were later known as the Alogi, apparently because they rejected the Logos doctrine of the fourth Gospel. In rejecting the Johannine doctrine, they also rejected the Johannine Gospel and the Revelation of John,

---

5. *II Clement* XII, 1.
6. *Didache* X, 5, 6. The last petition is a prayer for the coming of Christ. Cf. I Cor. 16:22.
7. *Adv. Trypho* LXXX. Cf. below, p. 158.

attributing both books to the Gnostic Cerinthus. In the first quarter of the third century, Caius, bishop of Rome, who opposed Montanism, attributed chiliastic doctrine to Cerinthus rather than to the Scriptures.[8] Irenaeus speaks of Christians who were considered orthodox but who were infected by heretical, i.e., by Gnostic views in that they denied a literal resurrection of the dead.[9] These views would of course eliminate any earthly millennial reign of Christ, which to Irenaeus is an important doctrine.[10] Origen, who, in his approach to Christian truth is more a Greek philosopher than a biblical theologian, opposed the literal interpretation of prophetic Scriptures, insisting that such literalism was "Jewish."[11]

One of the most vigorous opponents of chiliasm was Dionysius of Alexandria (died 265 A.D.). An Alexandrian bishop by the name of Nepos had written a book entitled *Refutation of the Allegorists* in which he defended millennial doctrine and attacked those who insisted upon the allegorical method of interpretation. Dionysius in his reply to Nepos, wrote,

> For that this was the doctrine which he taught, that the kingdom of Christ would be on earth; and he dreamed that it would consist in those things which formed the object of his own desires (for he was a lover of the body and altogether carnal), in the full satisfaction of the belly and lower lusts, that is, in feasts and carousals and marriages, and . . . in festivals and sacrifices and slayings of victims.[12]

Dionysius went on to say that although he did not understand the Revelation of John, he was sure that some deeper meaning underlies the language of the book, and that the interpretation

---

8. Cf. Eusebius, *H. E.*, III, xxviii, 1-2.
9. *Adv. Haer.* V, xxxi, 1.
10. *Ibid.*, V, xxxiii-xxxiv.
11. *De Principiis* II. xi.
12. Cf. Eusebius, *H. E.*, VII, xxv, iii.

of each passage is in some way hidden and more wonderful than appears on the surface. He then attacked the apostolic authorship of the Apocalypse, and by a comparison of the book with the Fourth Gospel insisted that it could not have been written by the same author.

This survey of early amillennialism makes it clear that its supporters did not have an alternate view of the kingdom of God which they felt was being set aside by a false teaching. They opposed chiliastic teaching either because they shared philosophical views which excluded it or because they reacted against the way millennialism was being taught by their contemporaries. No man before Augustine offers a creative interpretation of Revelation 20 other than the natural one. Furthermore, Justin Martyr tells us that chiliastic doctrine was practically normative and an essential element of orthodox doctrine. Justin was not a Jew, but a Gentile with a philosophical training whose mind would not be naturally attracted to Jewish apocalyptic. After admitting that he knows of true Christians who are not millenarians, he affirms, "But I and others, who are right-minded Christians on all points, are assured that there will be a resurrection of the dead, and a thousand years in Jerusalem, which will then be built, adorned, and enlarged, (as) the prophets Ezekiel and Isaiah and others declare."[13]   Harnack, one of the greatest masters of early Church History, says of this passage, "That a philosopher like Justin, with a bias towards an Hellenic construction of the Christian religion, should nevertheless have accepted its chiliastic elements is the strongest proof that these enthusiastic expectations were inseparably bound up with the Christian faith down to the middle of the 2d century."[14]

We are led to conclude that while there is evidence that not all Christians were millenarians, yet opposition was limited and the doctrine was very wide-spread. No other positive

13. *Adv. Trypho* LXXX.
14. A. Harnack, "Millennium," *The Encyclopaedia Britannica*, 9th ed.; XVI, p. 328.

interpretation is to be found before the time of Augustine; and the spiritual interpretation, when it appears, seems to be a new position and not the recovery of a teaching which had been lost for several centuries.

Chiliasm in Jewish apocalyptic

Can this prevalence of millennial doctrine be due to the perversive influence of Jewish apocalyptic? Professor Allis implies this when he asserts that "chiliastic views were extensively circulated in the Early Church through such Jewish or Jewish-Christian writings as *Enoch, 4 Esdras, Assumption of Moses, Ascension of Isaiah, Psalms of Solomon, Baruch,* writings which neither Jews nor Christians regarded as canonical.[15] The terminology must be more carefully defined before this statement can be left unquestioned. "Chiliasm" is commonly used in a twofold way, with a stricter and a looser meaning. In the strict sense, chiliasm, as its derivation indicates,[16] refers to the existence of a *temporal* earthly kingdom, in this case, of a thousand years duration. In this sense the word is strictly synonymous with "millennium."[17] It is not important whether the temporal kingdom is of a thousand calendar years' duration or not, and not all chiliasts would insist on a literal understanding of the length of the interregnum. It is in this sense that we use the term, to refer to the existence of a temporal earthly kingdom *per se.*

In this sense, it cannot be said that chiliastic views were widely disseminated in the early church by Jewish apocalypses, for the doctrine of a *millennium,* strictly speaking, is practically non-existent in Jewish literature known to antedate the New Testament, and the concept of a *temporal* earthly kingdom of any sort is found in only a few places. In *Enoch* 91-104, there is a temporal kingdom but of undefined duration. In IV *Ezra* 7:28, there is a kingdom which will last four

---

15. Oswald T. Allis, *ob. cit.,* p. 287.
16. From the Greek *chilias* meaning a thousand.
17. From the Latin *mille* meaning a thousand and *annus* meaning year.

hundred years.[18]   In the *Apocalypse of Baruch* 40:3, the kingdom is temporary but of undesignated duration.   In the *Secrets of Enoch* 32:1-2, there is a famous passage in which a millennial kingdom is usually found, but the language is not altogether unambiguous.[19]   Furthermore, this book may be of such a late date as to have little relevance for New Testament or early Christian eschatology.[20]

However, "chiliasm" has come to be used in a looser sense, not referring to a *temporal* kingdom as such or to its duration, but to the *character* of such a kingdom. The word has come to involve derogatory connotations and to indicate the "crass materialistic, sensualistic Jewish" interpretation of the earthly kingdom.   Some Jewish apocalypses picture an earthly kingdom of apparently eternal duration but primarily in terms of physical enjoyments.[21]   Thus while such books do not have a *temporal* kingdom at all, they are often described by the term "chiliastic," for the character of the kingdom is one of materialistic more than spiritual blessings.

---

18. 400 is the reading of the best textual authority. One Arabic source has 1000 years, but this is probably due to the influence of the biblical Apocalypse. Cf. G. H. Box, *The Ezra-Apocalypse* (London: Pitman, 1912), pp. 112-114.

19. "And I blessed the seventh day, which is the Sabbath, for in it I rested from all My labours. Then also I established the eighth day. Let the eighth be the first after My work, and let the days be after the fashion of seven thousand. Let there be at the beginning of the eighth thousand a time when there is no computation, and no end; neither years, nor months, nor weeks, nor days, nor hours." Cf. W. R. Morfill and R. H. Charles, *The Book of the Secrets of Enoch* (Oxford: Clarendon Press, 1896), pp. 45-46; cf. also Nevill Forbes and R. H. Charles in *The Apocrypha and Pseudepigrapha of the Old Testament* (Oxford: University Press, 1913), II, p. 451.

20. Cf. Kirsopp Lake, "The Date of Slavonic Enoch," *Harvard Theological Review*, XVI (1923), 397-8 where it is dated in the 7th century A.D. Cf. the discussion of the date of this book in H. H. Rowley, *The Relevance of Apocalyptic* (2nd ed.; London and Redhill: Lutterworth Press, 1947), pp. 95-96, and the literature there cited. Rowley concludes that the book probably lies well beyond the limits of the period of the Jewish apocalypses.

21. Cf. *Jubilees* 23, *Enoch* 1-36.

Christian and Jewish chiliasm

It is this latter meaning which Professor Allis seems to have in mind when he includes *The Assumption of Moses* and *The Psalms of Solomon* as the source of such views, for these books do not envisage a temporal kingdom at all, much less one of a chiliad of years. This very fact more sharply defines the basic issue which concerns us. We are not at the moment primarily concerned with the *character* of the millennial kingdom. Revelation 20 says only that Christ and his resurrected saints will sit on thrónes and reign. We are concerned with the *existence* of such a kingdom, whatever its character. It may be admitted that the character of the kingdom was sometimes interpreted in the Early Church in the light of Jewish apocalyptic largely in materialistic terms. It was this fact which caused the earliest revulsions against the millennial doctrine. This does not prove that the idea of the existence of a Christian millennium *per se* in Revelation 20 is a perversion of the truth because of Jewish influences. Such a kingdom might well be of very different character, the manifestation of the supernatural, "spiritual" powers of the kingdom of God and of the Messianic King, even in the physical realm, which would make it quite different from Jewish "chiliasm."

We may illustrate this by quoting from *The Apocalypse of Baruch.*

> And it shall come to pass when all is accomplished that was to come to pass in those parts, that the Messiah shall then begin to be revealed. And Behemoth shall be revealed from his place and Leviathan shall ascend from the sea, those two great monsters which I created on the fifth day of creation, and shall have kept until that time; and then they shall be for food for all that are left.[22]

---

22. 29:3-4.

Here is a description of the Messianic banquet with which the kingdom is inaugurated at the coming of Messiah, and it consists of feasting upon two huge sea monsters.

We have no biblical warrant to react so strongly to such exclusively materialistic portrayals of the messianic kingdom that we insist that the powers of the kingdom of God can have nothing to do with the physical world. This is essentially the issue. Can we have a millennium of earthly bliss at all without having the "crass, materialistic Jewish" type of kingdom?

Professor Vos has a brief but excellent discussion of the manifestation of the powers of the spiritual kingdom of God in the physical miracles of our Lord which suggests the solution to the problem. Professor Vos would not apply his own reasoning to a millennial kingdom, but the principle involved permits such an application. He faces the question of how the identification of the kingdom with the effects of a power working miracles largely in the physical realm is to be reconciled with the emphasis placed by Jesus upon the spiritual nature of the kingdom. The answer which Vos gives is that the physical evils which the power of the kingdom removes have a moral and spiritual background. Satan reigns both in the body of man and in his will, and the victory over Satan in the physical realm is symbolical of a similar victory in the spiritual. But this is not all. The physical signs have also a connection with the manifestation of the kingdom in the external sphere itself.

> The miraculous power is prophetic of that great kingdom-power which will be exerted at the end. It is especially in eschatological connections that a revelation of power is referred to, Matt. xxiv.30; Mk. xii.24. . . . It had to be shown immediately, that the work inaugurated by Jesus aims at nothing less than a supernatural renewal of the world, whereby all evil will be overcome, a renewal of the physical as well as of the spiritual world. Because the Old Testament had treated these two as belonging

inseparably together, and because in reality it would now appear that the two lay far apart in point of time, it was all the more necessary that some solid anticipations of the eschatological change should be given. . . . Here, as on other points, our Lord's teaching warns us against that excessive spiritualizing tendency, to which the external world becomes altogether worthless and indifferent or even withdrawn from the direct control of God.[23]

These words could well have been spoken by a millenarian; yet earlier, Professor Vos said, "What formally corresponds in our Lord's teaching to this notion [the Jewish "chiliastic expectation," "considerably tainted . . . by sensuality"] is the idea of the invisible, spiritual kingdom."[24]   The problem of the relationship of the spiritual, inward powers of the kingdom of God to the renovation of the heavens and the earth in the Age to Come, if this be thought of in physical terms at all, is different only in degree and not in kind from the relationship of those same powers to a temporal earthly kingdom.   The important point is the matter of emphasis, whether the material blessings are ends in themselves or merely manifestations of the spiritual. The concept of spiritual blessings and a spiritual world quite aloof from the material world is derived from Greek philosophical dualism and not from biblical theology. Surely the New Testament concept of the resurrection is not that of bodies consisting of spirit.   This is not the meaning of the "spiritual body."

The existence of a temporal earthly kingdom *per se* may not then be condemned because it is Jewish chiliasm. No essential problem exists if Christian eschatology has many points in common with Jewish eschatology. An analogous situation may be found in the fact that our Apocalypse as a whole has much in common with the genus of Jewish apocalyptic literature and

---

23. Geerhardus Vos, *The Teaching of Jesus Concerning the Kingdom of God and the Church*, pp. 97-98.
24. *Ibid.*, pp. 68-69.

is usually treated as such by liberal criticism. In fact, this is usually taken to be the solution to the problem raised by the book.[25] However, our Apocalypse has elements which set it apart from other apocalypses. It is not pseudonymous; it is thoroughly Christo-centric and soteriological; it portrays not the aloof, transcendent deity of the apocalypses far removed from the present troubles of his people, but the God of the New Testament whose love is active for man's redemption; in short, it is of a piece with the New Testament revelation and biblical theology.[26]

There is indubitable evidence that some early Christians interpreted the millennium of Revelation 20 in light of the Jewish apocalypses. Irenaeus quotes from the now lost fourth book of Papias' "Expositions of the Oracles of the Lord" words which Papias attributed to Jesus:

> The days will come, in which vines shall grow, each having ten thousand shoots, and on each shoot ten thousand branches, and on each branch again ten thousand twigs, and on each twig ten thousand clusters, and on each cluster ten thousand grapes, and each grape when pressed shall yield five-and-twenty measures of wine. And when any of the saints shall have taken hold of one of their clusters, another shall cry, I am a better cluster; take me, bless the Lord through me. Likewise also a grain of wheat shall produce ten thousand heads, and every head

25. Cf. A. M. Hunter, *Interpreting the N. T.* 1900-1950 (London: Student Christian Movement Press, 1951), pp. 97 ff. The *magnum opus* of this type of criticism is R. H. Charles, *A Critical and Exegetical Commentary on the Revelation of St. John* (New York: Scribner's, 1920, 2 vols.), an invaluable work for critical study. Charles has laid all subsequent scholarship under his debt. However, the water-shed in the interpretation of the Apocalypse is found in whether the book is treated as a baptized Jewish apocalypse, or as an inspired prophecy.

26. "Common sense and an uncorrupted taste rebel at placing in the same literary group [of the Jewish apocalypses] the Revelation of John . . ." Theodor Zahn, *Introduction to the New Testament* (E. T. Edinburgh: T. and T. Clark, 1909), III, p. 387.

shall have ten thousand grains, and every grain ten pounds of fine flour, bright and clean, and the other fruits, seeds and the grass shall produce in similar proportions, and all the animals, using these fruits which are products of the soil, shall become in their turn peaceable and harmonious, obedient to man in all subjection.[27]

These words are not found in the New Testament, nor is any language like them to be found. Very similar words occur in the *Apocalypse of Baruch*,[28] in fact, words so similar that some sort of interdependence must exist. Without doubt, Papias drew upon language from this Jewish apocalypse and attributed it to the Lord. This we may admit; but the fact in no way invalidates the natural interpretation of Revelation 20 because it is "Jewish." Papias' idea of the character of the millennium may have been Jewish but that does not invalidate the millennial doctrine *per se*. All it proves is that some early Christians *elaborated* the Christian doctrine of the millennium in light of a similar Jewish doctrine. It does not prove that all Christians have followed this procedure, nor does it prove that the doctrine itself, which admittedly has parallels in Jewish literature, is wrong and unbiblical. Our discussion of the exegesis of the verses concerned has endeavored to establish by inductive reasoning without reference to Jewish parallels that it is the only consistent interpretation.

The problem may be reduced to this: does the occurrence of a doctrine of a temporal kingdom in Jewish eschatology invalidate a similar doctrine in Christian theology? This is the crucial question. Such is the implication of those antimillenarians who would describe the millennial doctrine as "Jewish." What if a biblical millennium does find parallels in Jewish doctrine? All that is established thereby is that

---

27. Taken from Irenaeus *Adv. Haer.*, V, xxxiii, 3-4. Cf. J. B. Lightfoot, *The Apostolic Fathers* (London: Macmillan, 1893), p. 533.
28. Cf. R. H. Charles, ed.; *The Apocrypha and Pseudepigrapha of the Old Testament*, II, pp. 497-8.

there are certain close similarities between Jewish and Christian eschatology. It in no way invalidates the latter.

Parallels between Jewish and Christian eschatology

To insist that the natural interpretation of Revelation 20 is to be rejected because there are parallels to the Christian doctrine of the millennium in Jewish apocalyptic literature is to ignore the admitted fact that a similar parallelism is to be found in eschatological doctrines which are far more basic than that of the millennium. This brings us to the difficult question of the whole relationship between Jewish and Christian eschatology. Many conservative students have entirely neglected the study of these relationships. Much liberal criticism has gone to the extreme of insisting, like Schweitzer, upon understanding and interpreting the biblical eschatology consistently in the light of similar Jewish concepts.[29] Such a procedure leads to difficult problems. The insistence, for instance, that the Apocalypse of John finds its inspiration in the antecedent Jewish apocalyptic is faced by the amazing fact that while the Revelation is filled with bits of quotations from, references and allusions to the Old Testament, there is not a single distinct quotation from or reference to any non-canonical apocalypse.[30]

Between these two extremes there is a middle ground. Both the Jewish and Christian eschatology are based upon and find their roots in the Old Testament. Since this is an admitted fact, it would be quite amazing if there were not areas in which there would be found striking parallelism of concepts, even if the two streams of thought, although having a common source, were entirely independent in their development. That there is some sort of inter-relationship must be admitted; and

---

29. Cf. *supra* pp. 29ff.

30. R. H. Charles suggests a number of parallelisms, but these are not of such a character as to demonstrate dependence. Cf. *The Revelation of St. John*, I, pp. lxxxii-lxxxiii.

conservative biblical scholarship needs to give itself more carefully to the study of this area.

The most important illustration of this phenomenon, in the writer's judgment, is the concept of the two ages. Throughout the New Testament there runs what has been called the antithetical structure of eschatology: the antithesis of "this age" and "the age to come." The history of redemption is divided into these two periods, the present age in which we live and which will have its consummation at the Parousia of Christ (Matt. 24:3), and the age to come which will be inaugurated by our Lord upon his return from heaven. The antithesis is clearly seen in such passages as Matthew 12:32, Mark 10:30, Luke 20:34-5, Ephesians 1:21. The present age is dominated by Satan (II Cor. 4:4); it is an evil age (Gal. 1:4); it is characterized by concerns which choke out the message of the Gospel (Matt. 13:22); and the believer is not to conform to its standards and its interests (Rom. 12:2) because he has been delivered from its control (Gal. 1:4). The age to come will bring the full experience of the "powers" of God (Heb. 6:5), everlasting life (Mark 10:30), and a new order of existence which is entered upon at the resurrection (Luke 20:34-5).[31]

This distinct division of time into these two antithetical ages is not to be found in the Old Testament.[32] It is found, how-

31. The writer is aware of the problem which is raised by this antithetical structure for the existence of an interregnum between the two ages, i.e., of the millennial reign of Christ. Most of the references cited above make it appear that the age to come will follow directly upon the consummation of this age with no intervening period which must be required for the millennial reign of Christ. This is one of the strongest arguments in favor of the amillennial position, although it is infrequently used. However, there is an adequate solution to this problem which cannot be discussed in the limitations of the present work. It is suggested but not elaborated by Hermann Sasse in *Theologisches Wörterbuch zum Neuen Testament* (G. Kittel, Hsgbr.; Stuttgart: Kohlhammer, 1949), I, p. 207; and by Oscar Cullmann, *Königsherrschaft Christi und Kirche im Neuen Testament* (Zürich: Evangelischer Verlag, 1946), pp. 14-15.

32. Cf. the excellent discussion of the background of this concept in Geerhardus Vos, *The Pauline Eschatology* (Published by the Author, 1930, reissued by Eerdmans, 1952), pp. 1-20.

ever, in fully developed form in Jewish apocalyptic literature, especially in *IV Ezra,* a book written during the first century A.D.[33] So striking is this parallelism that we must recognize some sort of inter-relationship between New Testament and Jewish eschatological thought. Such an inter-relationship is recognized by Professor Vos, who has been known as a stalwart defender of the doctrine of divine revelation and the inspiration of the Scriptures,[34] and one of the outstanding adherents of a non-millenarian interpretation of the kingdom of God.[35] Vos says,

> That the formal contrast between the present age and the coming age was derived by Paul (or by Jesus) from that source [Jewish eschatology] has already been shown. . . . Of course, the Jewish eschatology has its basis in the Old Testament. This, however, can not wholly account for the agreement between it and Paul as to data going beyond the O. T. There is no escape from the conclusion that a piece of Jewish theology has been here by Revelation incorporated into the Apostle's teaching. Paul had none less than Jesus Himself as a predecessor in this. The main structure of the Jewish Apocalyptic is embodied in our Lord's teaching as well as in Paul's.[36]

This evident relationship between Christian and Jewish eschatology on the subject of the two ages dissipates entirely the force of the objection against the natural interpretation of Revelation 20 because it is "Jewish." If Professor Vos is right in saying that the New Testament revelation incorporates a piece of Jewish theology and one so basic to the structure

---

33. "For this cause the Most High has made not one Age but two" (7:50). "But the Day of Judgment shall be the end of this age and the beginning of the eternal age that is to come" (7:113) (G. H. Box's translation in *Apocrypha and Pseudepigrapha,* II, pp. 585, 590). Cf. the discussion in W.O.E. Oesterley, *II Esdras* (London: Methuen, 1933), pp. xxxi-xxxii.

34. Cf. his *Biblical Theology* (Grand Rapids: Eerdmans, 1948).

35. Cf. above pp. 56ff.

36. Geerhardus Vos, *The Pauline Eschatology,* pp. 27-8.

of New Testament eschatology as that of the two ages, there can be no valid objection on the part of those who follow Professor Vos' interpretation of the kingdom of God if there is a parallel in Jewish doctrine to the Christian teaching of the millennium; in fact, there could not even be a consistent objection if the New Testament eschatology should again embody a piece of Jewish eschatology in the stages by which this age is to pass away and the age to come be inaugurated, viz., by the agency of an interregnum of Christ on the earth.

After all has been said, however, the entire question of the "Jewishness" of such a millennial reign really has nothing to do with the interpretation of Revelation 20 and the application of the rules of hermeneutics to this passage. It has yet to be proven that the natural interpretation of the millennium was created by the influence of Jewish apocalyptic; for those who feel that it is due to Jewish influence, the illustration of the occurrence of the two ages in both bodies of literature should suffice to show that the objection has no weight. It also has yet to be proven that the spiritual interpretation was not *created* by Augustine as a substitute for the millennial interpretation, and that this spiritual interpretation is intrinsic to the book itself. Until this is shown, or until some more substantial objection is raised to the millennial interpretation of Revelation 20, it will have to stand.

THE SILENCE OF THE OTHER NEW TESTAMENT BOOKS

The second objection against the millennial interpretation of Revelation 20 which we are to consider is the evidence of the Gospels and the Epistles concerning this doctrine. It is alleged that if there is to be such a millennium, this teaching must have appeared in our Lord's teachings and in Paul's epistles. Since neither Jesus nor Paul seem to envisage such a millennial reign, it is held that we must interpret Revelation 20 in a non-millennial fashion, consistent with the silence of the rest of the New Testament.

The weakness of this objection

It must be granted that the one book in the New Testament which teaches the millennial interregnum is the Apocalypse. This however is no reason for rejecting the teaching. The implication is that a teaching which appears in only one writer or in only one part of the New Testament is to be rejected for that very reason.

This objection can hardly be sustained, and many who urge this principle against millennial doctrine are not consistent in its application. A most striking illustration is found in the usual amillennial interpretation of the parable of the leaven. One meets again and again the affirmation that the kingdom is essentially a hidden, growing principle which is gradually to extend its influence until it has brought the whole area of human life under its sway. Vos says, "It cannot be denied that Jesus here conceives of the kingdom as a growing organism, a leavening power, conceptions which will scarcely apply to anything else than to a spiritual order of things."[37] Allis asserts that "the usual interpretation, that that reference is here to leaven as illustrating the all-permeating and all-assimilating power of the gospel, is the only natural one."[38] Berkhof affirms, "Jesus . . . does not describe the influence of the Kingdom on science and art, on education and culture, on commerce and industry, and on our political and social life; yet there are plain indications in Scripture to the effect that its beneficent power is destined to extend to every department of life. . . . Jesus represents the Kingdom of God as a leaven, an all-pervasive force, destined to have a transforming influence on the life of the world. . . ."[39]

If this is the necessary interpretation of the parable, it is difficult to see how, logically, one is not led to the postmillennial

---

37. Geerhardus Vos, *The Teaching of Jesus Concerning the Kingdom of God and the Church*, pp. 56-7.
38. Oswald T. Allis, *op. cit.*, p. 88.
39. L. Berkhof, *The Kingdom of God* (Grand Rapids: Eerdmans, 1951) pp. 73-4.

position which finds in the Gospel of the kingdom the power that is so to permeate human society as to transform it and gradually to bring to pass the golden age when all the relationships of life have been brought into harmony with the will of God.

Be this as it may, it is notable that the parable of the leaven is the one proof text used to support this concept of the kingdom. The kingdom as a growing, permeating influence is not found elsewhere in our Lord's teachings; it does not occur in Paul; it is unknown in the Apocalypse. It may be said that the parable of the mustard seed teaches the same thing, the gradualness of the growth of the kingdom; but that is not the teaching of the mustard seed. It is the contrast between the insignificant manifestation of the kingdom of God at the first and the great thing the kingdom is to become.[40] The parable of the leaven similarly has been understood to teach something quite different about the kingdom than its all-permeating influence; like the mustard seed it teaches that the kingdom which at the beginning was manifested in such a tiny way that it was practically imperceptible would one day be all-enveloping in its sphere, without any indication as to how the latter end was to be gained.[41]

However, the fact that there is but a *single* proof text which can be used for this teaching, and that furthermore this one proof text is couched in parabolic language, without corroborative evidence from other parts of the New Testament, is never

---

40. The seed is used in Mark 4:26-29 to illustrate the supernatural power which characterizes the kingdom of God. There is nothing which man can do to "build" it or to bring about its growth. The kingdom is entirely the act of God and is extended by powers resident within itself. Man can only sow the seed; the rest is up to God. In both the parables of the sower and the tares, the metaphor of seed is used, but not to illustrate growth. Cf. above, pp. 127ff.

41. Cf. A. E. Barnett, *Understanding the Parables of Our Lord* (Nashville: Abingdon-Cokesbury, 1940), pp. 59-60; B. T. D. Smith, *The Gospel According to St. Matthew* (Cambridge: University Press, 1927), p. 139; Wilhelm Michaelis, *Das Evangelium nach Matthäus* (Zürich: Zwingli-Verlag, 1949), II, pp. 230-1.

a deterrent to that interpretation. This is singular, especially since the parable is quite susceptible to an altogether different interpretation.[42]

The evidence of the Gospels

We have already surveyed the evidence of the Gospels about the character of the future kingdom, and we need here only review it. We have seen that in our Lord's teachings, the kingdom is primarily futuristic and eschatological. While the powers of the kingdom have come into the world in the person and ministry of Jesus and men may now experience that kingdom as the spiritual reign of God within their lives and may enter into the kingdom as the realm of salvation, in the fullest sense of the word the kingdom is never said to have come; men will enter the fullness of its blessings in the future and are ever to pray for its coming.[43]

Furthermore the character of the future eschatological kingdom is often portrayed in terms that suggest that its scene is to be the earth though more often it seems to be placed in the age to come. We found that Jesus was much more concerned with the essential character of the kingdom of God, its ultimate consummation, and its relevance for man's life in the present

---

42. It should be said in passing that undoubtedly the kingdom of God has a social application. Many of the applications which have been made of the parable of the leaven are in themselves true, even though they are not explicitly taught in that parable. When God reigns in a man's life, *all* of the relations of his life are to be brought within the sphere of that sovereign will. If a "son of the kingdom" finds himself in business, he certainly must conduct his business in accordance with the will of God in his life. If a son of the kingdom is in politics, he will there endeavor to find God's will in that sphere of activity. Through persons who themselves are sons of the kingdom, the influence of the reign of God is extended into such social realms. This, however, is to be deduced from the teachings about the kingdom. To affirm that "whenever one of these spheres comes under the controlling influence of the principle of divine supremacy and glory, and this outwardly reveals itself, there we can truly say that the Kingdom of God has become manifest" may be logically correct; but it is to affirm more than the Scriptures directly teach. (Cf. G. Vos, *op. cit.*, p. 163.)

43. Cf. above, pp. 66-69.

than he was with the various aspects of its future manifestations.[44]   His great concern was that men would be led to make that irrevocable decision for the kingdom which would bring them into the present sphere of its saving power so that they would be prepared to enter the kingdom when it should finally come.   Everything else was subordinated to this end.

At this point we may recognize the prophetic perspective which sees many events lying in the future in terms of length and breadth but not in terms of depth.[45]   We may not be troubled by the absence of any millennial doctrine in our Lord's teaching, nor may this silence be used against this interpretation elsewhere; it was in no way relevant or essential to the immediate purposes of our Lord's ministry.

At one point, however, it is alleged that a contradiction is found between millenarianism and Jesus' doctrine of the kingdom which is so acute as to render the former untenable.   It is maintained that the kingdom established during a millennial, earthly reign of Christ involves a kingdom established and sustained by force, whereas our Lord's teaching envisages the kingdom as being established solely by the voluntary surrender of the hearts of men to the spiritual rule of God.   There is no room in such a concept for an earthly kingdom which is forced upon the nations of the earth.

Candlish objected to chiliasm because it implies

> that the perfect state of the kingdom of God on earth is to be attained, not by means of the agencies and influences now at work, but by a sudden supernatural interposition that ushers in a new dispensation, and breaks all continuity between the present and the millennial age.   The practical tendency of this is to lessen the motives and encouragements to work for the kingdom of God.   Since it is not to be brought to its success and triumph by the

44. Cf. above, pp. 69-73.
45. Cf. above, pp. 94-97.

loving efforts of Christians . . . but by the second coming
of Christ, Christian labour has not the encouragement of
hope, without which it can hardly be very strenuous and
persistent. . . . But, as we have seen, one of the chief
points in the teaching of Jesus about the kingdom of
God is its continuity, as a living principle, from its beginning inwardly and secretly without observation, till
its complete development and perfection in openly manifested glory.

. . . .

[The New Testament] describes a gradual progress of
the cause of Christ onwards to universal and complete
triumph in the end, as in Christ's parables of the Mustard
Seed and the Leaven. . . .[46]

More recent non-millennialists have not gone this far for
they have been compelled to recognize the strength of the
apocalyptic sayings in the Gospels concerning the future of
the kingdom.   Professor Vos, who, like Candlish, identifies
the kingdom with the church[47] still finds it necessary to admit
that the present "immanent kingdom as at first realized continues to partake of imperfections," and that the eschatological
crisis is necessary for two reasons: to bring the perfection to
the present spiritual kingdom, and to "supply this soul of the
kingdom with its fitting body," i.e., to bring about the regeneration of the outward physical world that it may become "the
natural and necessary instrument of revelation for the spiritual."[48]   Vos recognizes that the great kingdom-power is at
the end to be manifested in the external sphere when there will
ensue a supernatural renewal of the world, of the physical as
well as of the spiritual world, whereby all evil will be over-

---

46. James S. Candlish, *The Kingdom of God* (Edinburgh: T. and T.
Clark, 1884), pp. 336-7.

47. Cf. above, p. 57.

48. G. Vos, *The Teaching of Jesus Concerning the Kingdom of God and
the Church*, pp. 64-5.

come.[49] Even Professor Berkhof admits that the Gospel by
itself is not to establish the kingdom, but that supernatural
and catastrophic elements will enter into its establishment.[50]
Yet he protests vigorously against his understanding of the
premillennial position that the kingdom of God is to be established by force. If this were so, he says, Charlemagne and
the Roman Catholic Church at the time of the Reformation
were on the right track when they compelled men to accept
Christianity and burned heretics for the salvation of their
souls.[51]

It is however a caricature of the truth to affirm that this
power to be exercised in the future establishment of the kingdom is of the same order with the force employed by Charlemagne and the Roman Catholic Church. The New Testament
does indeed portray the future reign of Christ in terms of
force. When Christ comes again as King of kings and Lord
of lords, he will rule the nations with a rod of iron. (Rev.
19:15). This is judgment; but it is something more than
judgment. To those who have overcome and who have kept
his works will be given the same power over the nations, to
rule them with a rod of iron (Rev. 2:26). Christ is not to
reign alone; but the members of his Church are to share his
kingly authority over the world and over the kings of the
earth. This reign is to take place at the close of the present
age, as verses 25 and 28 indicate.[52] Only after the Lord
returns is there to begin the time of the ruling of the world
with the iron rod. This certainly affirms a "rule of force"[53]
of Christ and of his Church over the rest of the world whose
inhabitants do not yet belong to the Church.

---

49. *Ibid.*, pp. 96-7.
50. *Op. cit.*, pp. 158-9.
51. *Ibid.*, pp. 174-5.
52. The "morning star" indicates that the day is about to dawn. "In comparison to the day which will dawn with the future Parousia, the time of
looking forward to the Parousia is night." Theodor Zahn, *Die Offenbarung
des Johannes* (Leipzig and Erlangen: Deichert, 1924), I, pp. 294-5.
53. Zahn employs the word "Zwangsherrschaft" (*loc. cit.*).

This description of the future reign of Christ and his Church is to be realized in the period described in Revelation 20:1-6.[54] Here again the coming of Christ in glory and his subsequent reign are pictured in terms of military power. He comes riding on a white horse to make war, accompanied by the armies of heaven. But the instrument of conquest is the sharp sword that *issues from his mouth* (Rev. 19:11-16). It is hardly possible accurately to equate this sword used by the conquering Christ with the weapons used by Charlemagne and Rome. The military figures of speech are metaphors for the glorious power which the King shall exercise, and we may be sure that his glorious rule will be consistent with himself. This does not empty his coming and reign of their literalness or relegate them to the world of "spiritual," i.e., of non-spacial reality. He shall reign over the nations, on the earth, by an exercise of power and of force, but the weapons of his warfare may not be those of the earth. With this agree Jesus' words to Pilate, "My kingship is not of this world; if my kingship were of this world, my servants would fight, that I might not be handed over to the Jews; but my kingship is not from the world." The Revised Standard Version, from which we have here quoted, is correct in translating *basileia* by "kingship" instead of "kingdom." Jesus here is not referring to the realm over which he is to rule, but to the kingly authority which is his. This kingship does not derive its origin and character from this world. God's kingdom, whose mediatorial King is Christ, always operates by heavenly supernatural power. By such power was it revealed in the person and earthly ministry of our Lord; by such power is it now proclaimed; and by the same power, although manifested in a different realm, shall it be revealed in the time of his Parousia. It is the same supernatural power of God whether it be manifested in the quiet, inner work of the Spirit, or in the outward "rule of the iron rod." There is no reason why the sovereign power of God

54. So Zahn, *loc. cit.*

through Christ may not be realized in more than one realm: in the present spiritual realm of salvation, and in a future outward manifestation upon the earth. The futuristic apocalyptic element of the Gospels is inclusive of the latter.

Berkhof himself would differentiate between the *regnum gratiae,* over the Church, and the *regnum potentiae,* over the universe. The latter designates God's authority over the world which prevents it from frustrating his purposes in the *regnum gratiae,* and by which it becomes subservient to the interests of the Church.[55] It would seem as though we should go a bit further than Berkhof does in his description of the *regnum potentiae.* Paul tells us in Philippians 2:9-10 that every knee is to bow and every tongue confess that Jesus Christ is Lord to the glory of God the Father. Unless this indicates universal salvation, it means that Christ's mediatorial ministry will ultimately bring all intelligent beings to his feet, all of them in recognition and confession of his Lordship, but not all in voluntary submission. This seems necessarily to involve force applied in the moral and spiritual realm.

It is in similar terms that Paul describes the interregnum; he is to reign until he has *subdued* all enemies (I Cor. 15:20-23), that he may finally surrender the kingdom to God. This involves more than grace and more than judgment; it involves the power of the reign of Christ subduing those who are unwilling. This is one of the main purposes of the millennial reign, and it is difficult to see how there can be any valid objection to it.

The evidence of the Epistles

When we turn to the epistles of Paul, we find no teachings which exclude a millennial reign. While in a number of references, the kingdom is a present, spiritual reality,[56] for

---

55. L. Berkhof, *Systematic Theology* (Second revised and enlarged ed.; Grand Rapids: Eerdmans, 1941), pp. 406-411.
56. Rom. 14:17; Col. 1:13.

the most part it is future and apocalyptic, something yet to be inherited. In one passage in particular, Paul seems to have an interregnum in mind. "For as in Adam all die, so also in Christ shall all be made alive. But each in his own order: Christ the first fruits, then (*epeita*) at his coming those who belong to Christ. Then (*eita*) comes the end, when he delivers the kingdom to God the Father after destroying every rule and every authority and power. For he must reign until he has put all his enemies under his feet" (I Cor. 15:22-25). Both *epeita* and *eita,* the words used here, are adverbs of time, denoting sequence. There is a temporal adverb used of con-current events, *tote;* but this word is not used in this passage. *Eita* by itself in the New Testament ". . . as in classic Greek . . . stands in enumerations, to mark a sequence depending on temporal succession. . . ."[57] The Authorized Version is mis-leading in translating, "Christ the first fruits; afterward they that are Christ's at his coming. Then cometh the end . . . , " for in a sequence like this, *eita* as well as *epeita* means after-ward. This may be seen by Paul's use of the same adverbs earlier in the chapter: ". . . he appeared to Cephas, then (*eita,* i.e., after that) to the twelve. Then (*epeita,* i.e., after that) he appeared to more than five hundred brethren at one time . . . then (*epeita*) he appeared to James, then (*eita*) to all the apostles" (I Cor. 15:5-7). Here Paul enumerates a series of events which took place one after the other. Similarly, in discussing the resurrection, he has in mind a succession of events which may be translated: "But each in his own order: Christ the first fruits, after that at his coming those who be-long to Christ. After that comes the end, when he delivers the kingdom to God the Father. . . . For he must reign until he has subdued all enemies." When Paul wrote these words, some thirty years had elapsed since the resurrection of Christ,

---

57. J. H. Thayer, *A Greek-English Lexicon of the New Testament* (New York: American Book Co., 1889), p. 188. Cf. further in H. G. Liddell and R. Scott, *A Greek-English Lexicon,* revised by H. S. Jones, (Oxford: Clarendon Press, 1940), I, p. 498.

"the first fruits"; and though at times Paul seems to anticipate the imminent return of Christ, at other times he has a
long historical perspective (Rom. 11).

One may reason, therefore, that the "end"[58] is to take place
at a considerable period after the Parousia of Christ, at which
time (at the end) he will deliver the kingdom to the Father
when, by means of his reign during the intervening period, he
has completed the task of subduing all enemies.[59] While Paul
does not speak of a *millennial* reign of Christ, the precise exegesis of his language leads to the conclusion that he does have
in mind an interregnum of undefined duration. He indicates
that some period will elapse after the Parousia during which
Christ is reigning before the end when he finally turns the
kingdom over to God. Professor Vos, who rejects the chiliastic interpretation of this passage, concedes, "It must be
granted that, had the Apostle meant to express such a thought,
eita would have been entirely appropriate for the purpose."[60]

The burden of Vos' argument against the millennial interpretation of this passage is the time of the *terminus ab quo* of
Christ's reign. If his reign begins with the Parousia, there
must be an interregnum; but if the reign begins at the Ascension, the *telos* may be so closely subsequent to the Parousia as

---

58. For the present purpose, it is not important whether the end (*telos*)
refers to the end of the resurrection, i. e., the resurrection of the dead who
are not Christ's, or to the end of Christ's reign. In either case, the *telos*
will occur *after* the Parousia and the resurrection of Christ's disciples.

59. An interregnum in the mind of Paul in this passage is recognized by
Henry St. John Thackeray, *The Relation of St. Paul to Contemporary
Jewish Thought* (London: Macmillan, 1900), p. 121; Johannes Weiss, *Der
erste Korintherbrief* (Göttingen: Vandenhoeck and Ruprecht, 1910), pp.
358-9; and *The History of Primitive Christianity* (E.T.; New York:
Wilson-Erickson, 1937), II, 532; Hans Lietzmann, *An die Korinther I. II*,
Handbuch zum Neuen Testament 9 (Tübingen: Mohr, 1923), pp. 81-2;
Philipp Bachmann, *Der erste Brief des Paulus an die Korinther* (Theodor
Zahn, Hsgbr.; 2 Aufl.; Leipzig: Deichert, 1910), pp. 438-440; Oscar Cull-
mann, *Christ and Time* (E. T.; Philadelphia: Westminster Press, 1950)
pp. 67, 151: H. A. W. Meyer, *Critical and Exegetical Handbook to the
Epistles to the Corinthians* (Edinburgh: T. and T. Clark, 1881), II, pp.
59-63.

60. Geerhardus Vos, *The Pauline Eschatology* (Published by the Author.
1930, reissued by Eerdmans, 1952), p. 243.

to be practically identical. He concludes, "all we can say is that there is nothing in the words of the passage itself, nor in Paul's general teaching, to hinder us in dating this period of eschatological conquest from the Saviour's death and resurrection."[61] However, this does not settle the matter. Christ may have entered into his mediatorial reign at the Ascension — this we believe — and yet anticipate a greater realization of his mediatorial power over the world after his Parousia. The mediatorial reign of Christ may well include the present age and the millennial age, with both ages involving the exercise of the same kingly authority in two different realms — over his Church, and over the world at large.

It is true that in I Corinthians 15:50-58, the resurrection of the righteous and the very last "end" fall together.[62] But this is because the Apostle here speaks in terms of absolute consummation, as Vos himself says.[63] Paul, like our Lord, is far more concerned with the ultimate outcome, and with the immediate application of it than he is with the stages by which the consummation is realized. The force of the line of reasoning based on I Corinthians 15:23-26 is that Paul is not concerned with the stages by which Christ's ultimate triumph is achieved; he is concerned with the certainty of that triumph *whose realization is assured because it has already begun.* The language which indicates that Christ's reign will extend beyond this period between the Parousia and the *telos* is quite incidental to his purpose, but is all the more significant for that very reason.

The objection that Paul does not differentiate between the kingdom of Christ and the kingdom of God as he should have done in verse 50 if he had a temporal reign of Christ in mind after the resurrection,[64] loses its force when it is remembered that Paul nowhere consistently makes such a distinction. Ac-

---

61. *Ibid.,* p. 245.
62. *Loc. cit.*
63. *Loc. cit.*
64. *Ibid.,* p. 246.

cording to the non-millennial interpretation, he should make such a distinction between the present age — the kingdom of Christ, and the future age — the kingdom of God. This he does not do. The kingdom of God in this present age (Rom. 14:17) is also the kingdom of Christ (Col. 1:13), and the future kingdom involves both the kingdom of Christ and of God (Eph. 5:5). In fact, if anything is to be made of this terminology, we should conclude that there is yet to be a mediatorial kingdom of Christ, after the Parousia. According to I Corinthians 15:24, at the *telos* Christ will give over his kingdom to his Father, and from this we might assume that thereafter, strictly speaking, there would be no kingdom of Christ. Yet in Ephesians 5:5, the kingdom of Christ is a future inheritance;[65] and in II Timothy 4:1 we find the kingdom of Christ coupled with his appearing (*epiphaneia*) and his judgment of the living and the dead. However, this is a point which cannot be pressed.

Progressive Revelation

Our survey of the Gospels has led to the conclusion that they contain hints of a future earthly kingdom; and we have found in Paul the definite suggestion of a reign of Christ between the Parousia and the *telos*.

However, even if this evidence did not exist, even if the rest of the Bible were entirely silent on this point, that fact would not militate against the belief in a millennium if the exegesis of the Apocalypse required it. Divine revelation within the Scriptures is not static but progressive. The implications of progressive revelation are always applied in the study of the relationship between the New Testament and the Old and within the movement from Moses to the post-exilic prophets in the Old Testament writings. There is no reason why there might not be a further application of progress in revelation in

---

65. For the meaning of "inherit," cf. I Cor. 6:9, 10; 15:50; Gal. 5:21. It is an eschatological concept.

the New Testament books. It might well be that in the Apocalypse, elements of a new revelation were imparted to John by the Lord, to the effect that there should be a millennial interregnum.[66]

CONCLUSION

The Old Testament looks forward to the manifestation of God's kingdom primarily in terms of its eschatological consummation. The kingdom is usually seen established on the earth; but sometimes the vision goes beyond the earth into the age to come (Isaiah 65:17, 66:22), when there will be new heavens and a new earth. However, these two stages of the future eschatological kingdom are not clearly differentiated in the Old Testament.

In the Gospels, there is scarcely more distinction made between the earthly kingdom and the eternal kingdom. The future perspective for the most part envisages the *ultimate* fulfillment of the kingdom whose powers were manifested in the historic mission of Jesus.

Paul in one place goes a bit further to indicate his expectation of an interval between the Parousia and the *telos;* but his interests are quite soteriological and individual, and he gives little attention to the larger manifestation of the kingdom of God.

In the Revelation — the one prophetic book of the New Testament — the relationship between the earthly and the eternal kingdom is made clear. For the first time, Scripture teaches that there is to be an interregnum, a temporal earthly kingdom, which precedes the final eternal age to come of the new heavens and the new earth. Paul indeed suggests this interregnum, but his words are not as explicit as is the Revelation. For the first time, it is clear that the resurrection is to

---

66. So Theodor Zahn, *Die Offenbarung des Johannes,* II, p. 600.

take place in two stages; a resurrection of the saved before the millennium and a resurrection of the unsaved at its termination.[67]   The fact that the relationship of these events which will see the consummation of God's kingly rule is made explicit for the first time only in the last verses of the last book of the Bible should pose no acute problem to those who believe in progressive revelation.

The basic question remains: What does the exegesis of Revelation 20 require?   All other considerations must be subservient to the exegesis of this passage.

---

67. There are passages elsewhere that hint at such a partial resurrection (Luke 14:14, 20:35, I Thess. 4:16, Phil. 3:11, I Cor. 15:23) or a resurrection in two stages (Daniel 12:2, John 5:29).

INDEXES

Indexes

Index of Subjects

Index of Authors

Index of Biblical References, etc.

192

Early Christian Literature

Printed in the United States
93791LV00002B/171/A

Made in United States
Troutdale, OR
01/06/2024

16754767R00119